Footprints from the Past

Henry J. Schut

Kashan Publishing
Delano, Minnesota

Lives of great men all remind us
We can make our lives sublime
And, departing, leave behind us
Footprints in the sands of time

Footprints, that perhaps another
Sailing o'er life's solemn main
A forlorn, shipwrecked brother
Seeing, shall take heart again.

from Psalm of Life by Longfellow

This book is an attempt to record the footprints left by my ancestors and to provide a look at those added by Hazel and me. Others may not wish to follow them, neither do I necessarily ask that they repeat our way. It is my hope that, pondering the paths our footprints have made, they may learn and leave even better paths.

It is also my prayer that others may see in our life that "Jesus led us all the way," even though we didn't always walk in His way.

Henry J. Schut

Acknowledgements

The Schut family wishes to thank the following people for their time and effort spent preparing Henry's manuscript for publication:

Carroll Schultz, who advised Henry during the writing of this project and acted as a preliminary editor.

Carol Frick, who edited the final manuscript.

Linda Hanner, who wrote the back cover text and handled the publishing.

Foreword

It was so like Henry to make light of what he had written. But, he did put a lot of work and much of himself into assembling the information for this book. A "pain in the neck"? I don't think so. We all know there is bad that goes with the good.

However, he has omitted telling of the many responsibilities he accepted and fulfilled for his church and community. He has not told of the help and encouragement he has doled out in such generous portions wherever he saw the need. If the number of prayers he has sent to God through Christ won't match that of the most devout Christian, I'm sure his sincerity would more than balance the scale. There is no doubt about his love of Jesus Christ, of his family or of people in general.

Henry died at Mt. Sinai Hospital. Henry had not written everything he had wanted to say, even though he did write page after page while he was in the hospital for tests and awaiting what turned out to be his last operation, a triple by-pass in his heart.

Because he was so faithful at recording these many dates and happenings of and for his family, I felt it was only fitting that these notes be made about him. His long obituary that was printed in the local newspapers attests to the busy life he led. It was as follows:

Henry J. Schut, 70, of Rt. 2, Maple Lake, died May 6 at Mt. Sinai Hospital, Minneapolis.

Funeral services were conducted at 11 a.m., May 9, at Silver Creek Reformed Church, Silver Creek, with Rev. Carl Boersma officiating. Burial followed at Lakeview Cemetery. Silver Creek Twp. Friends called from 4 to 9 p.m., May 8, at the Dingmann-Ferrell Funeral Home, Annandale, with a prayer service at 8 p.m.

Survived by: wife - Hazel of Maple Lake, six children - Dr. Lawrence (wife Loretta) of Minneapolis; Wayne (wife Joyce) of Rochester; Mrs. John (Marilyn) Lee of St. Cloud; Mrs. Ed (Darlene) Scott of Seattle, Wash.; Mrs. Douglas (Linda) Foster of Wyoming, Mn.; and Mrs. Charles (Lois) Bakker of Rockford. One brother - Bert of Escondido, Calif.; and 17 grandchildren.

Preceded in death by two brothers, Dr. John and William; and one sister, Elsie.

Henry Schut was born June 5, 1910, in Silver Creek Twp. to the late John and Jennie (Mol) Schut.

He farmed in Silver Creek Twp. for 30 years. He graduated from St. Cloud State University in 1964 and taught at Maple Lake High School for 10 years. He received Teacher of the Year award at Maple Lake in 1970. He received the WCCO Radio Good Neighbor Award in June of 1964.

He was a member of the Silver Creek Reformed Church and served many years as consistory member and Sunday School teacher at the church. He was a member of the General Synod Executive Committee of the Reformed Church of America.

He was a member of the Governor's Council on Developmental Disabilities, past board member of Wright County Retirement Center in Buffalo, and past board member of Land O' Lakes, Inc.

He was a member of the Executive Committee of the National Ataxia Foundation and had served as president for 10 years. He authored the book *Ten Years to Live* in 1978.

Memorials are preferred to the National Ataxia Foundation.

Pallbearers were Dr. Lawrence Schut, Wayne Schut, John Lee, Ed Scott, Douglas Foster, and Charles Bakker.

Honorary pallbearers were Karleen Anderson, Bert Plaggerman, Jim Plaggerman, Roy Plaggerman, Julie Schuur, and Bud Vandergon.

Organist was Orma Lou Jacobsma; and vocalists were Julie Anderson and Connie Mol.

I'd like to add that Henry was a real friend. It has been a true privilege to work with him on this book.

If I were asked to write an epitaph for him it would have to be:

Henry J. Schut
June 5, 1910—May 6, 1981
He put his heart into everything he did.

Good-bye, Henry. You were loved,
Carroll Schultz

Contents

Part I

Across the Ocean

Part I

Preface

In recording the legacy left to us by our ancestors from across the ocean, it is important that the life and customs of our forebears be included. It is equally important that this knowledge be accepted as part of our Holland heritage.

Part I is a record of one family's struggle to get to America, their failures and their problems. The names of Chris Dykstra, Anna and the rest are fictional. However, many of the main events are based on true stories as they were told to me. A number of the details and observations are, out of necessity, products of my imagination and cannot be accepted as the actual wording or actions that took place.

These characters represent people who really did live and die as their story portrays. The feelings they express were experienced by many immigrants from Holland as they left their native land to come to America.

A good share of them left in anger and vowed never to return to the oppression and poverty from which they had come. Their gratitude to America for the opportunities they found here have been expressed hundreds of times to me and to others.

Many immigrants who came from Holland were wealthy, and came for different reasons. That is not the story of our family's heritage. This story is representative of only my ancestors, who were poor peasant folk.

The Holland of today is not to be judged by the contents of this story, as it is much different from the Holland my grandparents fled in such desperation.

1

Building a Dream

Chris Dykstra swings his large scythe with the steady firm stroke of a man who has spent many years in these hayfields of Gelderland, Holland. He stops briefly to wipe the sweat from his eyes and forehead. He looks over the great field of waving grass that still awaits the scythe. At the far end of this field, he sees the fine home of Herr Soest Dyke. A few rods beyond that stands the two-room shack where he and his wife, Anna, now live. He doesn't call it a home, because it was a calf barn until he and Anna moved into it. "But," he will admit, "it has sheltered us from three years of rain and cold. And the small stone walls have kept the kitchen-living room above freezing. And Anna manages quite well in keeping the rooms clean."

His thoughts are suddenly broken when the large dinner bell of Herr Soest Dyke peals out time for the midday meal. He looks across the field of uncut grass with a sigh. He had contracted with Herr Soest Dyke to cut it for a guilder. By working hard, he can finish the task in one day and will have earned a whole guilder. He sets the scythe on its handle and takes several swift strikes of his whetstone against the blade to restore its razor-sharp edge.

Chris takes great pride in being able to cut a clean, even swath. His muscular body swings back and forth rhythmically with each swish of the scythe. When he arrives at the edge of the field nearest his home, he sees Anna coming with a platter of food. She is also carrying their daughter, who will soon be four years old. Rika is old enough to walk, but the sharp grass stubble would scratch and even pierce her tender little feet. Her parents have not yet acquired enough money to buy her a pair of *klompen* (wooden shoes). Chris has been making some small ones for her during his spare time, but there has been very little of that. As Anna draws near, Chris hastens his pace. He is hungry and thirsty and needs a break.

"Am I glad to see you," Chris says as a greeting.

"I'm sorry I'm a little late, but the potatoes wouldn't get done over that slow peat fire," explains Anna. "I do have a surprise for you though," she beams. "Vrouw Soest Dyke came out and sent a cup of coffee for you."

Anna offers the cup to Chris adding, "It isn't very hot any more, but the weather will keep you warm enough, I'm sure."

"And Daddy," adds Rika, "Mama let me carry your bread all the way out here."

Chris smiles through the dust and sweat on his face. "That is a good girl. With the potatoes and bread and a whole cup of coffee, I will have enough food till evening. I hope you will bring me some water during the afternoon," he adds, turning again to his wife.

"That I will do gladly for my loving husband," she replies. Then frowning a bit, she complains, "I wish you would buy a little meat or eggs to eat. You are so insistent on saving every cent you earn that I'm afraid you will lose your strength. What little beef soup we have is not enough."

"I know you feel I am very thrifty," Chris says between mouthfuls of food, "but you know the reason is a good one."

"I do know," she agrees, "but if you starve yourself, you won't live to use the money."

Watching him sitting there in the dusty stubble and gulping his food down, she cannot keep the tears from coming.

"You work so hard," she pleads. "And I'm so afraid our dream won't come true."

"Now don't you fret. Hundreds of us poor people have had a new beginning and I won't let you and Rika live like our parents have had to. Besides, it burns me up to work so hard while this Herr Soest Dyke gets rich on our constant toil. I'll show him we don't have to work for him for bread and potatoes!"

Chris rises abruptly. "I must keep going if I am to finish this field." He squeezes Anna's hand and takes Rika in his arms, kissing her lightly before returning her to her mother. Anna drains the last drop of coffee onto her tongue. Her *klompen* keep time with the "swish—ish, swish—ish" of Chris's scythe as it fades away behind her.

The shadows are long as Chris swings the scythe up over his shoulder and trudges wearily toward Herr Soest Dyke's back door. He knocks and Artje, the maid, opens it. She is short and a little heavy for her height, but Chris likes her. She is always friendly and flashes a wide smile at him. Sometimes she quietly slips him a package of leftover food from the master's table.

"May I speak to Herr Soest Dyke?" Chris asks.

"I'll ask him if he wants to see you," she replies. "He has been gone nearly all day and seems either tired or just quiet, but I'll ask him."

She disappears into the house while Chris stands outside the door. He can see the handsome furniture and beautiful Delft dishes and arrangements standing on the shelves along the walls of the dining room. They must have cost hundreds of guilders. His eyes move from side to side. Everything is beautiful and expensive.

There have been times when Chris has felt like taking his strong fists and sweeping those beautiful, delicate china dishes off the shelves and sending them crashing to the floor. He has to eat from wooden plates and clay cups. His bitterness burns near to fury. Herr Soest Dyke and men like him could take away even their dark bread and potatoes whenever they might choose. Chris knows he is powerless against the social system in which he lives.

His thoughts are suddenly interrupted as Herr Soest Dyke steps through the door, asking brusquely, "What do you want?"

It is not easy for Chris to squelch his feelings, but he replies with control. "I've finished cutting your field of hay and would like to have my wages."

"Are you finished already? I thought it would take you most of tomorrow, too. However, that is good. I will pay you. The agreement was one guilder, wasn't it? Those are very good wages for a day's work. I shall have to bargain with you more shrewdly next time." With that he takes out his wallet and gives Chris a silver guilder and turns to go into the house.

"Herr Soest Dyke!" calls Chris. "Do you need anyone to haul up the hay and pile it? I will be able to do that for you in three or four days when it is dry."

"I have a man coming to do that, but it would go faster if he had help. I offered to pay him 75 cents per day and if you want to help him I will pay you that also because I know you are a hard worker. Let me know tomorrow morning, will you?" With that he slams the door shut.

While Chris walks the short distance to his house, he is angry and bitter. "Herr Soest Dyke could have been a little more considerate," he mutters under his breath.

As he nears the little house, he sees Rika running to meet him and his whole face lights up in a smile. She runs to him and clamps her small arms around his legs as he swings the scythe high up on the limb of a tree. His strong arms lift her above his head and set her on his broad shoulder. She giggles and laughs and says, "Now jump, Papa, and give me a fast ride to the house. Mama has supper ready."

"That's good," he says. "I'm very hungry."

4

"Did you finish the field, Chris?" Anna asks as he comes through the door.

"Yes, and I have a whole guilder to add to our secret treasure!"

"Not all of it," Anna counters. "We must buy some food."

"Well, spend only a little. And maybe I will be able to cut hay for Herr Bronk the next two days. And then help put up the hay I cut today for Herr Soest Dyke. How much do we have saved now?"

"I think it must be nearly 50 guilders," Anna says. Chris's bitterness and anger have melted away by the time he sits down to eat. "Now, Rika, fold your hands while Papa prays."

Chris asks God to bless their food and prays for forgiveness for the anger and bitterness he had felt just a few minutes before. The potatoes and turnips taste especially good. It is the little fat and butter in them that Anna had received from Vrouw Soest Dyke for her cleaning up the yard and garden. The extras also helped to add taste to the dark rye bread Anna had baked.

The last of the setting sun comes through the window behind Rika and she watches its reflection in the small cup of buttermilk that her mother had brought for her also from the Soest Dyke farm.

Though it is near dark as they finish their meal, Chris pulls the well-worn Bible down from its shelf and reads a chapter out of it. Then he thanks God for health, home, and family.

After Rika has gone to bed, Anna takes a letter out of the pocket of her long apron and gives it to Chris.

"It's a letter from brother Bert in America," she says. "I can't read it very well. Maybe you can tell me what it's about."

"Let me see it," he says. "My army service did help me read, but that is about all I can say for the time I spent there."

He holds the letter close to the window to catch the few remaining rays of light and reads slowly:

Dear Chris and Anna,

It is now nearly two years since I deserted the Dutch army to sail for America. What a change has come to my life. I can work every day and the employers let us eat with them at their table. We have meat, vegetables, bread and milk every day and as much as we want. I hope to be able to rent a farm for myself sometime and have my own livestock and family. America offers me so much! I hope all of our family can come here.

I loaned brothers Hendrich, Jake, and Chris some money to come here and maybe by next summer we can all get enough money together to loan to you so you can sail for America, too.

We have already arranged to bring Father and Mother over later this summer. Mother is in such poor health, she shouldn't have to live her last years there in Holland.

It isn't an easy trip and it takes weeks on the boat, and then two or three days by train from new York to where we are. You cannot imagine how large this land is! America goes thousands of miles further west and there are millions of acres of land for free. I think you will like it here as there are many people here from Holland. We have Dutch church services and nearly everybody talks Dutch in our little town.

If you decide to come, let me know how much money you need and we will try to help you come next summer.

Your loving brother,
Bert

Chris is so excited he can hardly read the last few sentences.

"Just think, Anna!" he almost shouts. "All we can eat! Even meat! We must save all we can. Then next summer we can tell old Soest Dyke to cut his own hay!"

"Hush," cautions Anna. "Next summer is still many months away and we can't tell what will happen before then. I'm so grateful for my wonderful brothers. They even want my mother and father to come to America. We must thank

God for this promise of help and learn to be patient."

"Yes, but I can hardly wait. It's going to be a happy day when I can tell old Soest Dyke I don't need him anymore."

The darkness soon brings Chris and Anna back to reality. A long chilly winter still lies ahead. Their weary bodies are soon asleep and the morning light brings another day of toil.

The days go by swiftly and winter brings different problems. Chris is able to find work at a dairy farm a mile away from home where he is offered five guilders per week and a quart of buttermilk and five pounds of meat each month. The ground that Anna had been offered for a garden in return for her also taking care of Vrouw Soest Dyke's garden produced good crops of carrots, turnips, and potatoes which will keep quite well in the hole under the kitchen floor. With careful planning, they are able to save nearly another hundred guilders by spring. If brother Bert can lend them another 75 guilders, they will have enough money to sail to America. But they will have to take a boat carrying freight.

"It might even be possible for us to earn enough to pay for our food on the boat. If we can find the right boat at the right time," Chris speculates, raising his arms in hope toward heaven.

Chris and Anna buy a large steamer trunk, build a few boxes from some rough boards, and make plans to go to the closest harbor to take a ship to America.

Chris doesn't dare tell Herr Soest Dyke until he is sure of his plans. He has been thinking for many months about when and what he would say when he quits. A broad smile spreads across his face every time he thinks about it. He will really tell him off!

Chris writes Anna's brother Bert that they will need about one hundred guilders more than their savings. On April 15, Bert's letter arrives with the money. The day has come! Their dream is coming true!

"Herr Soest Dyke," says Chris one evening after work, "next Monday we are leaving for America. I won't need to work from dawn till dark for a lousy guilder per day. In America, we will get good wages and plenty to eat. Anna's brothers are there and they have a place for us to live. We are saying good-bye to Holland forever!"

"Chris Dykstra!" comes the stern reply. "You are a good worker. You have a secure job here. There are many problems along the way and many folk never even arrive in America. You are making a grave mistake. You will always have food and shelter here."

The years of near hate for this man well up in Chris's heart. Herr Soest Dyke has never done a hard day's work in his life and has squeezed out every minute of labor from his employees for starvation wages. Chris's eyes flash as a pent-up torment of words comes unrestrained from his lips. He points his calloused finger within inches of Herr Soest Dyke's nose and growls, "You call potatoes and turnips and that shack we live in food and shelter? I could work for 50 years for you and I'd never know what it means to have a warm home and enough meat and milk for my family. You spend more money on one hand-painted urn in your house than you pay me in a year. I'd be lucky if my children learned to read and write, while yours are riding in a beautiful buggy to a special school to learn how to oppress my children and grandchildren! I've had enough! My faith in God will help me find a new and decent life for us and our children in America. Good-bye, Herr Soest Dyke, and may God have mercy on your soul! Because my Bible says 'Woe to you who oppress the poor!'"

With mixed feelings, Chris stalks away from the stunned and angry farmer. His training in Christian faith tells him he should not leave a fellow man with such hate in his heart. Yet, he has to admit he feels good. It seems as though the weight of all the words he has ever wanted to say to the old Herr have

suddenly lifted from his mind and heart. Try as he might, he
can feel no regret.

2

The Dream Vanishes

Anna's sisters have helped her pack most of the few possessions she and Chris plan to take with them. Many of the remaining things Anna has given to friends and relatives. Chris, Anna, and Rika are to stay with Anna's sisters for a few days before they take the train to Amsterdam, about 50 miles away, where they are to book passage on a freighter sailing for New York.

Anna finds it difficult to think of separating from her sisters. The thought of never seeing them again nearly overwhelms her. Yet, she knows the decision has been made and Chris is determined to go.

The evening before their departure, Anna shares her feelings with Chris.

"I have such a heartache about leaving here," she confesses. "Isn't there any way we can make a decent living here?"

"Anna," he replies, "I feel so strongly about going to America that I will go alone if you won't go with me. Then when you want to come, I'll have a home for you."

"Oh, no!" she replies quickly. "You mean more to me than anything else in the world. I'll never mention it again."

They embrace each other and Chris holds Anna very close to him.

"I know you will be happy in America," he assures her. "Remember, your brothers and father are there already."

"I am a little concerned about the trip across the ocean. You know Bert's last letter said that Mother had a stroke on the ship and only lived for some months after she arrived in America. Those ships are very unhealthy. But, I will go wherever you go."

"We will ship our boxes to my parents in Zaandam near Amsterdam first, until we can find a ship going to America. Now let's get some sleep. We have many plans for tomorrow," Chris says.

The trip to Zaandam proves to be very interesting. Anna has seldom been away from her hometown and this is Rika's first train ride. There are many stops. The lush green flatlands of the country with cattle grazing in the pastures and the large windmills turning in the wind remind them of their home and Anna cannot help thinking, I'm leaving this forever. But as the miles roll by she resolutely sets her thoughts on the land to which they are going. America, a land of promise.

They arrive at Chris's parents and are greeted with great affection from both young and old.

Chris's brother encourages him, "If you find you like it, maybe we will come, too!"

The next day, Chris and Anna go to the seaport to find a freighter going to America on which they can book passage.

Chris and Anna have never seen so many people. People speaking strange languages among many large boxes, machinery, produce, and lumber, some being hauled from ships to storage, others being carried back onto the ship. It all seems utter confusion to this couple from the hinterlands of Gelderland.

"I wonder where we have to go to get tickets," says Chris to Anna.

"I have no idea," she replies. "There's a man near the door over there. Why don't we ask him?"

Together they walk toward the man. "Excuse me, Herr, do you know where we can buy tickets to travel to America on one of these ships?"

"Oh yes," he replies. "Come with me into another building and I'll show you where you can get them."

"That's very kind of you, " Anna says appreciatively. "We are from the country and we are rather dumb when it comes to buying things in a busy place like this."

"That's understandable," the man replies. "I was born in the country near Arnheim, in Gelderland, and it took me a long time to find my way around here. By the way, my name is Nick Cloo. What are you names?"

"I am Chris Dykstra and this is Anna, my wife," replies Chris.

"I thought you were from Gelderland because of your style of clothes. What part of America are you planning to go to?"

"Oh, I have four brothers and my father who live in Iowa and they are helping us to get started," volunteers Anna.

"That is really nice of them. It is so nice to have someone you know when you get there," says Nick. "The trip across the ocean can be very rough sometimes. Maybe I can get you a place on a larger ship. They usually sail more smoothly and have better quarters for people like you."

"Oh, that would help a lot," Anna tells him. "My mother became very sick on the trip to America and only lived seven months after she got there."

"That is too bad. I'm sorry to hear that," Nick says, sounding so very sympathetic.

Chris walks close to Nick and studies his face. His dealings with friendly strangers have not always been good and something tells him to be cautious.

They climb an old stairs to an old office on the second floor. The name on the desk is "New World Freight Lines," a firm that Chris has heard about, and his suspicions are eased.

There is no one at the desk, so Nick says, "Just sit here for a minute and I'll try to find the agent."

They seat themselves on the bench along the wall and a few moments later Nick reappears to say, "The agent will be busy for a couple of hours, but he said he has room for you on his ship. It will be sailing for New York next week. Do you have any children? He doesn't want many children on this trip."

"We have only one daughter. She is four years old and we will watch that she will not be any bother," Chris promises.

"That's good!" says Nick. "The agent said he charges one hundred guilders for each adult and 25 to 50 guilders for each child, depending on the age. That includes food and a place to sleep for each of you. Since your daughter is only four years old, she will go for 25 guilders. How does that sound to you?"

"That is very reasonable," says Chris.

"If you will give me the 225 guilders, I will give you a receipt for the money and I'll get the tickets from the agent. That way you can go home sooner. I'll also find out when and where you can bring your trunks and boxes so they get on the ship. Also, when and where you will have to get on the ship."

Nick writes out a receipt and gives it to Chris and Chris counts out his hard-earned guilders into Nick's hand.

"It will take about 15 minutes to get all the tickets ready. I'll come back and give them to you and you will be all set to go."

"I'm surely glad we found Nick," sighs Anna. "It would have taken us all day to get a ticket."

"Yes," agrees Chris, "I didn't trust him at first, but we have this receipt, so we can always show that. And we should be back in Zaandam before dark."

The 15 minutes pass quickly and they begin to watch the door where Nick had gone through. A half-hour and still no sign of Nick. An hour passes and Chris knocks at the door. An old man appears and says, "What do you want?"

"Do you know where Nick Cloo is?" asks Chris.

"Nick Cloo? I never heard of him," replies the old man.

Fear and anger grip Chris as he tells the old man what has

happened. Meanwhile, Anna comes running up to the door. The old man looks at them sadly and says, "That happens around here a lot. I'm afraid you have been swindled. You'll never see your 225 guilders again. This building has many exits. Your so-called Nick Cloo is probably miles away. Your receipt is worthless."

"Can't you call the police?" asks Anna.

"Yes, but there are thousands of people here in Amsterdam and the police don't know where to look. Besides, I sometimes think the police aren't too interested in helping poor people from this country."

Chris is burning with anger, but there is no one on whom to vent his anger.

"I didn't trust him at first," he fumes. "Why did I give him the money and let him out of my sight!"

He turns to Anna in despair. "Just think. Years of work and food savings all gone! Our dream of America is gone! All gone, Anna, all gone!" he shouts.

Anna cannot speak. She is crying uncontrollably. They return to the straight wall-bench and both sit, holding each other, weeping bitterly. The old man slowly closes the door on a scene he has witnessed before.

Chris suddenly sits up. "This crying is not going to bring back that money. Lucky we didn't give that Nick all our money. We can start again. We did it once. We can do it again!"

"How? And where? Are you going back to Gelderland and work for Herr Soest Dyke again?" asks Anna.

"No! Never!" vows Chris vehemently. "I'll find work here near my family in Zaandam. I am still strong. I know I can work harder than most men. I'll get work. I know I will."

He stands up, straightens his back and together they walk out of the door, down the creaky stairs and up the narrow streets toward Zaandam.

It isn't easy to tell their story to Chris's brothers, but they are sympathetic and promise to help Chris and Anna find a home and some work.

Rika cannot understand the turn of events. "Aren't we going to America?" she asks, looking from her mother to her father.

"Not now," says Chris. "But we will. We will, my darling. We won't give up that easily."

After a few days, Chris finds work with a farmer about 20 miles away. Herr Ver Doorn owns a large farm and employs several men. He expects a lot of work from his employees, but pays and treats them well. He finds a small home for Chris and Anna and soon they are settled in. Having picked up the few necessities to eat and to sleep, they give thanks to God that their belongings hadn't disappeared, too.

Chris has always worked hard, but now, after being swindled out of his opportunity to go to America, he works like a man possessed. Earning and saving money once more become an obsession. Herr Ver Doorn responds with better pay and more and harder work for Chris. Chris sleeps little and seldom takes time to visit. His only rest time is a part of Sunday when there are no necessary chores.

The rest of the summer and winter speed by and every possible guilder and cent go into the large crack under the floor.

One spring evening Chris asks Anna, "How much money do we have saved up?"

Anna has been keeping a record of it mentally and answers, "I think we have nearly 150 guilders. But, Chris, we must have some clothes. Rika is going to school soon and she will need a coat and a dress."

"I wonder if my sisters' children have any dresses that would fit her. Or maybe you could make them over to fit?"

"That means we will have to go there to find out, and you haven't had enough time to take off to see them since we left there a year ago. I know my sisters in Oldebrook would have some. But that is a day's journey by train. The fare to get there would cost as much as the clothes would if I bought them here."

"Maybe you should visit my sisters in Zaandam," Chris offers. If they don't have any used ones, they can help you find some in Amsterdam."

"How much money can I spend?" asks Anna.

"As little as necessary. I will trust you for that. You know how hard I work to earn it and how hard you try to save. The quicker we have the four hundred guilders it will take now, the quicker we go to America. And we are going if it kills me."

"Oh! Don't say that, Chris. I'd rather live in poverty for 50 years than have you kill yourself working just to get to America."

Chris's face becomes firm and his eyes glare. "Well, not me! I believe God wants us to raise our family in a land where we can be free from these slave drivers here in Holland. I know Herr Ver Doorn is better than Herr Soest Dyke, but he really doesn't care about us. He treats us better because he knows I will work harder. He still is trying to get as much work out of us as he can. He is not fooling me."

"It may take us another year or two before we have enough money to go to America. And the way you are working, I don't know how you can take it," counters Anna.

"Oh! I know I'm not as young anymore, but I'm as strong as I ever was. We will make it." Then he adds emphatically, "You can bet Chris Dykstra will go to America! He will never give up!"

Anna turns quietly away toward the door. She doesn't want him to see the tears rolling down her cheeks. She just knows that going to America means more to Chris than life itself, and it makes her fearful.

The days grow longer and it is hay cutting time again. Chris spends day after day swinging his scythe. Herr Ver Doorn sometimes slips Chris an extra guilder for finishing his work ahead of schedule. Chris appreciates it and works that much harder.

By Friday afternoon, Chris has cut hay every day since Monday. There are blisters on both of his hands and he is tired. It is very hot and humid. His head aches. But he will work till nearly dark to finish the field. He grits his teeth and swings into the task at a furious pace.

In a nearby field the other workers are piling up hay in small piles so the hay will cure better before hauling it to a large stack by the barn. They all admire Chris's ability to work and have developed a deep respect for this seemingly tireless machine.

Suddenly, one of them sees Chris pitch forward into the uncut hay and lie still. They run over to him. A quick look indicates that Chris is undoubtedly dead. One of the workers runs to Herr Ver Doorn's home and shouts out the bad news. "Chris Dykstra is lying in the hayfield! He looks like he's dead!"

Herr Ver Doorn immediately calls the police. They come very quickly and verify that Chris is indeed dead. As they bring Chris's body to the shade of a tree on the lawn, the policeman says, "I suppose we should tell his wife. Where does she live?"

"His wife and little daughter live about a mile down that road. It's a small green house on the right side," volunteers one of the workers.

Herr Ver Doorn looks at the policeman and waves his hand at him. "You tell her, will you?" Then, looking at his workers standing around, he says, "Maybe you should go back to piling up that hay. It looks like it may rain."

The policeman isn't too pleased with his task, but it is part of his job, so he walks slowly up the narrow road to the little green house.

He doesn't see anyone, so he knocks at the door. Anna opens the door and steps back in surprise to see the officer.

"Vrouw Dykstra?" he asks.

"Yes."

"Well," he blurts out, "your husband dropped dead in the hayfield." Then, realizing how harsh that had sounded, his voice softens and he adds, "We carried him to Herr Ver Doorn's lawn." A pause, then he asks, "What do you want us to do with him?"

Anna looks at the officer in utter disbelief. "What did you say?"

Irritated at having to make the difficult announcement a second time, he almost shouts, "Didn't you hear me? I said your husband is dead! What do you want us to do with him?"

Anna's eyes go wild. She flies at the officer, screaming, "You killed him! You killed him!" She scratches his face, tears into his hair and kicks and hits him again and again.

The surprised officer grabs at her arms and clamps them behind her. He half pushes and half throws her into a chair in the kitchen.

"You crazy woman!" he hollers. "I didn't kill him. He dropped dead in the hayfield. I didn't have a thing to do with it!"

Little Rika hears the commotion from her play yard behind the house. She comes running in the door just as the officer is shouting at Anna, "Now you just stay in that chair before I choke you!"

"What happened, Mama?" cries Rika. Then she shrieks at the officer, "What are you doing to my mama?"

The officer ignores her and stamps off to the door. He turns around and points a stubby finger at Anna, commanding, "You stay right there until I call Pastor Van Beck. Maybe he can talk some sense into you." With that, he breaks into a run toward the local village church.

Rika races across the room and flings her arms around her mother's neck. "What happened, Mama? What's the matter?"

Anna pushes her away, showing no recognition. She sits

staring into space, mumbling, "He said he would go to America if it killed him. . . Even if it killed him." The words kept tumbling out in a blurring, incoherent manner. No tears, no wailing, no sorrow was evident. Just staring in disbelief.

The workers on the Ver Doorn farm nail a box together of boards purchased from a local mill, then gently lay Chris's body into this makeshift casket. The next day the pastor and a few friends lay Chris's body to rest in a hurriedly dug grave in the cemetery where hundreds of unmarked, forgotten men and women have been buried.

Chris's relatives are notified and come to comfort Anna. But she speaks to them only in monosyllables, or ignores them completely. She performs some of her household duties in a machine-like manner.

At times she will pick up Rika to rock her, but there is no lullaby. Instead, she mumbles softly, "Lord, why did you let him die? Why?"

Other times, as she rocks her little girl, it is, "Now, what will Rika and I do? Lord, what will we do?"

Chris's brothers beg Anna to come with them, but their pleadings fall on deaf ears and on a mind that has been nearly destroyed by the shock.

"Mama and I will stay here. I'll take care of her," volunteers Rika. "And Pastor Van Beck will help us, I know he will."

The brothers are at a loss to know what to do. Pastor Van Beck speaks up, "Why don't you leave her here for a while with Rika. I think she may recover better in familiar surroundings than if we force her to move at this time. I'll ask the local authorities to bring her food and I will let you know what happens."

Since no one has any better idea, they reluctantly follow his advice. Chris's relatives return home with heavy hearts. Pastor Van Beck goes to the local charity society and explains the situation, but the story of the "crazy woman" has already spread through the village. No one wants to volunteer to bring her food.

"Herr Bakker," says Pastor Van Beck sternly, "it is your Christian duty to care for that woman. I expect you to bring her food, water, and anything she may need. And remember, she has that little daughter living with her. I want all of you to show concern for her."

He looks at the group in the room and speaks sharply. "Remember, Vrouw Anna is still a child of God. We must care for her while she is recovering from her sorrow."

The following day Vrouw Bakker gives her husband a kettle of hot potato soup and cautions him to be careful and not get too close to Vrouw Dykstra.

"She is a strong woman," she warns. "And she has table knives. She could injure you. Besides," she adds in a whisper, "I think she may have a devil in her!"

Herr Bakker needs no coaching from his wife as he already has decided on a course of action. He takes the hot kettle of soup and a long-handled hay fork from the barn, then hikes quickly up the road. When he comes near the little green house he calls out, "Vrouw Dykstra! Vrouw Dykstra! Open the window of your kitchen!"

The window opens slowly and a wild, haggard face appears. Then Rika peeps around her mother cautiously, as Herr Bakker approaches.

"I have something for you to eat," he says apprehensively. "You can take the kettle off the end of this fork where I'm hanging it. You empty it into your kettle and place my kettle back on the fork teeth."

He watches intently, and adds the warning, "Don't you come out of that house or I'll drive this fork into you!"

Mechanically, Anna does as she has been ordered. Herr Bakker retreats with a sigh of relief. The window closes slowly.

During a week of watchful care, Peter Van Beck visits Anna often. He takes his wife, Freida, with him several times, but

Anna just stares at the two of them with wild, seemingly unseeing eyes. Her tongue speaks only occasionally, and then in nonsensical words. Her one touch with reality comes as she places her arms around Rika and pulls the little girl onto her lap. Rika is puzzled. She is very happy to see Pastor Van Beck and chatters with him and Freida nearly constantly.

Pastor Van Beck looks around the room and at Anna. The usually neat room is in disarray, with dirty dishes and kettles sitting on the floor as well as all over the table and on chairs. Anna's hands and clothes are soiled and Rika's dress looks as though she has not taken it off even to go to bed.

Pastor Van Beck (or Dominice Van Beck, as he is also called) is a minister of the large prestigious Hervormde Kerk in the village. Being used to moving about in the elite circles of his congregation with ease and self-confidence, facing this new problem is difficult and awkward. His heart goes out to this poor peasant woman whose mind seems to have become deranged by the death of her husband. He is also concerned about her attractive little daughter. He knows that soon the owner of the house will be evicting them. He knows too that no one else will accept them into their home. And apparently even her relatives are not able or else not willing to cope with this distraught woman.

"How sad it is," he says to Vrouw Freida as they walk slowly away from the little green house.

Vrouw Freida turns and waves a friendly good-bye and Rika calls in answer, "Good-bye. Please come back again. Very soon?"

"What can we do?" asks the pastor, hardly loud enough for Freida to hear. "What must we do?"

"One thing is sure. They can't stay there for very long," sighs Freida.

"If there were only some place they could be together. It seems that the child is the only person she will respond to. Yet, we can't leave the child in her care, either."

"Our church has a beautiful orphanage where Rika can go. The caretakers are really caring people. They will train her well in Christian doctrine and behavior. It's really a fine place," Freida says, trying hard to believe this to be the best solution.

"Yes, I've thought of that, but what would happen to Anna?"

"I really don't think it makes much difference, does it? She doesn't seem to know what is going on, or even to care. I think her mind is practically gone."

"That may be, but she is still a child of God. We must show our love and care for her. Besides, she may recover."

"I have my doubts. The state institution in Amsterdam has so many like her. They just go on and on like machines, or maybe I should say like animals."

"I know that is true, but there ought to be a better way to treat people like Anna who have been hurt so deeply that their minds get sick. Everything in me says that it is wrong. Yet, very few agree with me."

"Listen to me," urges Freida. "You can't let your feelings ruin your better judgment. Anna must go to an institution and Rika to the orphanage. You know there is no choice."

"At the present, there isn't. But I hope and pray that sometime, sometime, we will all care enough to help people like Anna instead of locking them up. To separate this daughter from her mother at this time of sorrow will guarantee that the mother will never be well again."

"So, what is your solution now?"

"I have no other," he concedes dejectedly.

The next Monday morning Vrouw Freida and Vrouw Hendrickje DeLoof from the Hervormde Kerk orphanage come to take Rika to the orphanage.

Chris and Anna's dream has vanished forever.

3

Broken Minds, Broken Hearts

Vrouw Freida's words of confidence had been well founded, for Vrouw Hendrickje DeLoof had been chosen to direct the Hervormde Kerk orphanage because of her ability to manage the institution and her way of instilling behavior habits in the children entrusted to her care. And she takes her tasks seriously.

She is short and could be called a little stout. Her sparkling blue eyes are set in a round face which invariably breaks into a smile at the sight of a child. Her deep love for children and strong Christian faith not only shine from her face, but are evident in all that she does. She loves it when "her" children shorten the Hendrickje to "Hennie."

On the morning that Vrouw Freida introduces Hennie to Rika Dykstra, she has already told Hennie all about the problems of the Dykstra family and about the decisions that have been made in regard to Anna and Rika. Hennie has not been in complete agreement of the decisions, but she holds no authority to change them or even to question them. That is done by her superiors.

Hennie hopes to be able to persuade Rika to go with her without making a scene involving Anna. How to do this is still uppermost in their minds when they arrive at the little green house.

Rika sees them coming and runs out to meet them. She recognized Vrouw Freida and is glad to see her.

"Rika," says Vrouw Freida, "this is Vrouw Hendrickje

DeLoof. She has a home with many little girls and boys who live with her. She wants to learn to know you."

Rika holds tightly to Vrouw Freida's long skirts while she studies Hennie's face. Rika is by nature an outgoing child, but the experiences of the last week have aroused her suspicions about the behavior of strangers.

Hennie stoops down and holds out her hands, explaining quietly, "Yes, my name is Vrouw Hendrickje DeLoof, but my children call me Hennie for short. You may call me that, too, if you like."

Rika makes no response.

"Did you have breakfast yet?"

Rika shakes her head and says, "No, Herr Bakker didn't bring us any today."

Hennie's heart goes out to this lovely little girl whose hands and face are dirty, whose hair is uncombed, and who is wearing a very soiled dress that is not buttoned right. There is an attraction that radiates from this child making Hennie want to fold her in her arms. Instead, she reaches into her purse and takes out two small biscuits. Holding them out toward Rika, she says, "Here, you may eat these. They were baked this morning."

Rika steps slowly forward, takes one and eats it hungrily.

"Do you like it?"

Rika nods.

"Why don't you sit on the grass here by me and eat the other one?"

"That's a good idea," says Vrouw Freida. "And I will go to the house and see your mother."

Rika obediently sits beside Hennie, grasping the biscuit as though it were the only thing in the world that was hers. Hennie places her arm around Rika and draws her close. Rika looks up at her and, after a fashion, smiles.

"How would you like to come with me and play with the boys and girls that live in my home?" Hennie asks cautiously.

Rika frowns. "What if Papa should come back and I'm gone?"

"Do you think he might come back, Rika?"

"I don't know. The pastor said Papa was in heaven. Can't he come back from there?"

"I'm afraid not, Rika."

"But I want him to come back! I want to talk to him. Mama can't talk. Papa sometimes would tell me stories from the Bible. I remember one story where a man named Lazarus became alive again because Jesus was there and he could make people alive again. Can't that happen now? I wish Jesus would come now. Maybe he could make Mama talk again, too."

"So do I," says Hennie devoutly. "But it may take some time."

There is a long silence of closeness between the two of them, then suddenly Hennie exclaims, "Do you know what? We have a papa for all our children! And he tells stories to all the boys and girls. Would you like to come to my home for a couple days and visit us?"

"What about Mama? Can she come, too?"

"Not now. She is sick and must go to a place where they can make her well. When she can talk again, maybe she can come to see you, or else we can take you to see her?"

Vrouw Freida has been sitting with Anna while Hennie and Rika had their little talk. Anna has not given any indication of having seen or heard her. Suddenly Rika comes running into the house to her mother's side. She shouts excitedly, "Mama! I'm going with Vrouw Freida and Hennie for a visit. There are lots of other girls and boys there. And even a papa who can tell me Bible stories!"

Anna frowns a moment, but seems to have lost all contact with the world around her. Even the care she showed for Rika the day before has vanished.

Freida and Hennie walk rapidly down the road with Rika between them. They have no desire to witness the scene they know will happen when the officers come to move Anna to her new "home." Anna knows nothing about what lies ahead. The future of Rika is also uncertain.

The orphanage is well staffed and the needs of the children are met by substantial gifts from the church. Clothes and food are adequate and many widows and single girls play games and care for the social needs of the children. Attendance at a Christian day school is a requirement and catechism classes teach each child the fundamentals of the Christian faith.

When Hennie takes Rika into the home it is nearly noon. The children are coming into the large dining hall from school. The excitement and noise nearly overwhelm Rika. She tries to hide behind Hennie's skirts. She makes a move to run away toward home, but Hennie's hand is clamped around her little wrist, gently but firmly. She cannot get away. When the children see Hennie they quiet down immediately. Rika has been washed and dressed in a crisp new dress, making her feel different, too. Vrouw Hendrickje raises her hand and speaks to the group.

"Children," she beams at them, "this is Rika Dykstra. She is coming to visit us for a few days. If she likes it here, she may stay."

Lifting Rika up in her arms, she says, "Say hello to Rika."

"Hello, Rika!" they all shout.

Then Hennie places Rika next to a friendly girl named Aaltje and helps dish up her food. Soon Rika is lost in conversation and the fun of the group.

The first few days and nights are very difficult for Rika. She does enjoy the story time with Papa DeLoof, but she cries herself to sleep pleading for Mama to come.

After two weeks, Hennie makes arrangements to take Rika to visit Anna in Amsterdam. The visit is disappointing to Rika. Anna is sitting in a chair when she sees Rika run to greet her.

"Mama, Mama!" Rika cries, "I'm so glad to see you. Are you better? Can you talk to me?"

A brief smile crosses Anna's face, then the fearful blank expression returns. She takes Rika's hand listlessly into her own, but there seems to be no sign of love or concern for the daughter she and Chris had loved so dearly.

"Mama," Rika cries, "I want to sit on your lap. I want you to hug me and kiss me. Can't you even look at me?"

Who can express the hurt of a seven-year-old daughter who has lost the love and concern of her mother? thinks Hennie as tears stream unashamedly down her face.

"Come, Rika," says Hennie. "Mama is still too sick to see or hear you. Maybe next time she will be better."

Rika learns to adjust quickly after her visit to her mother. She learns her lessons easily and is a willing helper to Hennie and Herr DeLoof. Months soon add up to years and at age 16 Rika is working in the homes of the community as a maid. She has many friends in the church and sings in the choir. It seems as though the trauma of her young life has made a sensitive, concerned young lady of her.

At 18, she meets and falls in love with a young man named Jon Brink. He is not a really healthy person, but he does possess a keen mind. He has had a good education and comes from a good family. Their love ripens into a commitment to be married. At last, life is being kind to Rika. They are to live in a nice home and Jon is offered a good job. But Jon's health begins to fail rapidly and shortly before their wedding date, Rika says good-bye to Jon forever. She weeps bitterly over his death. Her faith in a loving God is being tested as never before.

"Why Lord, did you take him from me? I needed him so much."

Vrouw Freida Van Beck tries to comfort her, but Rika will not be comforted. Vrouw Freida has never been known for her care and concern. Impatiently, she rebukes Rika, "Listen, Rika, what about Jon's mother? Jon was her only son. She won't ever have another son. You can always find another boyfriend. There are many of them."

"That's easy for you to say," cries Rika through her tears. "You don't hurt like I do. You can't know what Jon meant to me. There is just not another Jon Brink. You don't understand!" With a quick turn, she looks hard at Vrouw Freida and adds, "And you never will!" With that, Rika runs distraught from the room.

4

Joy Mixed with Tears

Rika is not a young lady who will spend her days feeling
sorry for herself. She has inherited some of her father's
determination and persistence. Her life in the orphanage has
fostered a strong sense of dependence on her own abilities.
Also, her daily training in the Christian faith has developed
within her an acceptance of life's circumstances, even when
they bring sorrow and grief. If doubts come, they are
dispelled when she remembers Hennie's constant assurances
that God loves his children even when people and events cause
hurts.

Rika continues to work in the homes of the community
where her attractiveness and personality soon draw the
attention of several new suitors. At first, the hurt of having lost
Jon causes her to ignore any thoughts of commitment to any
other man. But, as time begins to heal these deep wounds, her
interest becomes centered on a young man named Albert
Nykerk.

Albert has been trained to work as a cobbler in his father's
shoe shop. Making special shoes for wealthy people and
repairing worn ones for the middle class society is considered
a lucrative occupation and carries a certain amount of
prestige. Peasants and servants usually wear wooden shoes, but
to make shoes for the aristocracy demands a high degree of
expertise and experience.

Albert is impressed by the independent, attractive young
lady that Rika has become. After a short but aggressive
courtship, he persuades Rika to become his wife. The marriage

is not only prompted by respect and admiration, but a deep love that is based on mutual commitment to God.

The shoe shop is not the most healthy place for Albert to be spending his time. The long hours he has to put in do not allow for much exercise or exposure to fresh air. However his business grows so rapidly that he soon hires a man to help him keep up with the growing demands for his workmanship.

The front of the shop is directly on the street where passersby can see the craftsmen working at their benches. The living quarters are behind the shop, opening onto a small alley where only a few spears of precious grass grow between the cobblestones paving the walk-way.

The contrast between Rika's childhood in the country and this crowded city life is striking. Fortunately, Rika's time in the orphanage and her work as a maid have helped her adjust to this change.

It just takes time, Rika tells herself.

The closeness of Albert's work to his home makes the home life of Rika and Albert a happy one. Albert is always happy to introduce his lovely young wife to his customers and Rika soon learns to help keep the shop clean and attractive.

One evening Rika says, "Albert, I think I have a happy secret to share with you."

"Oh?" he asks nonchalantly. "What is it this time?"

"We are going to have a baby!" she shouts as though to make sure the whole world will hear the good news.

Albert jumps from his chair, picks her up in his arms and exclaims, "Isn't that great? Just think. I will be a papa!"

Rika laughs with genuine happiness as she kisses him and embraces him.

"Yes, and I know you will be a good papa. And I know you would like a son. We will pray for that, won't we?"

"Of course, and we will name him Bert, after my father. Papa will like that."

"But it could be a girl," teases Rika.

32

Albert frowns, then smiles. "If it's a girl, we will name her Anna after your mother."

Rika's face clouds and she begins to weep quietly. "How I wish she would get well. She always loved children so much. I can't forget how she looked at me when I visited her last year. There wasn't one single indication that she recognized me. Even when I explained who I was."

"Maybe when the baby comes we can show it to her. It may even bring back her memory."

"I'm afraid that after all these years there isn't much chance of that. The caretaker told me she acts like she has no mind of her own. She does only what she is told, then stands or sits staring into space."

Rika pauses momentarily before continuing, "I shall never forget that police officer coming into our home and telling Mama that Papa was dead. He didn't show any more feeling than if our dog had died. Maybe not as much."

"I think people care a little more now, don't you?" Albert comments.

"Sometimes I do. I know that Herr DeLoof in the orphanage did. He was like a father to me. He seemed to love and care for everybody."

"What makes people so different?" Albert ponders.

"Oh, I'm sure the love of Jesus that people have in their hearts makes the difference. I really believe Pastor Van Beck was a loving man, too, but somehow he couldn't let people see that he cared." Rika frowns and adds, "I don't think Vrouw Freida had much feeling, though. She was so wrapped up in acting how she thought a pastor's wife should act that she forgot what it means to love."

Albert has never heard his sweet Rika vent her feelings like this before. Now he realizes that the deep hurt of rejection and sorrow are not completely healed. He holds her close, strokes her forehead and wipes away the tears that are flowing like rivulets down her cheeks.

When he feels she has had enough time to work through her grief, Albert coaxes Rika with, "Come, Dearest, we do have good news. Let's go tell my father and mother. They will be really excited. Their first grandchild!"

Rika wipes her face and smiles. "That's right," she says, still half crying. "Forgive me for spoiling this happy occasion."

"Yes, of course," replies Albert. "I'm glad you could share that deep hurt with me. I think your tragic experiences have made you a very caring person. That's one of the things I love about you."

Albert's parents are very dear to both Rika and Albert, so it is with much joy that they share the hope and expectations of their first child with them.

The months go by rapidly and they are happy times. Rika feels God is being good to her. Albert and she dream of the time when they can have a real home of their own, with a flower garden and a small lawn where their children can run and play, and where Albert can get a chance to breathe some fresh air.

There is one fear that lurks in Rika's mind. It is Albert's constant cold. He seldom complains about it, but there are times when his severe coughing spells cause her memory to go back to some of the friends she had at the orphanage. Immediately, she forces herself to turn her thoughts to happier things.

The baby boy arrives in January. What a joy! Albert can hardly contain himself. He literally dances around the room when he is told.

The baby is baptized "Bert" as Albert had wished and the Nykerk family rejoice, giving praise to God for His blessing.

Little Bert grows slowly and cries often. Each cry brings Albert out of the shop. He takes the child from the crib and tries to comfort him until he falls back to sleep. On one of these occasions Rika remarks, "I wish Bert would grow a little faster and not have such a cold so much of the time. He seems a little weaker and paler than he should be."

"Oh, I wouldn't worry about it, Rika. My mother says I was not a strong baby at first, either. He will get better and get more color when we can get him out in the spring sunshine."

"Just the same, I would like to take him to the doctor. And another thing, I think it's about time you went to see a doctor, too. Your cough isn't getting any better. And you are getting thinner. I can tell by how your clothes fit."

"You remind me of my mother. Always worrying about my health. I've always been thin."

"But I don't like that constant cough," insists Rika. "I heard coughing spells like that in the orphanage and I don't like them."

Albert flushes a little and replies, "If Bert isn't improved in a week, we'll take him to the doctor. Does that make you feel better?"

"Some," says Rika. "But promise me you will go with me and I'll feel better yet."

"All right," he responds with resignation. "You are an insistent wife. Now I must get back to the shop."

Albert walks into his shoe shop and closes the door behind him. He sits down at his bench, but before he can pick up his work his whole body convulses in a spasm of coughing. Rika's heart doubles its pace. She can no longer submerge her fear. Those coughs she had heard too often at the orphanage usually meant—she hardly dares to think of the word, but it screams inside her heart—tuberculosis!

"No, no, Lord, not my loving husband!" she cries in anguish. "We are so happy. And he is such a kind, considerate person. Not him, Lord, please, not him."

She buries her head in the bed pillow and weeps. Suddenly she hears little Bert crying and coughing. A thought stabs her consciousness. Could he have it too? She flings the thought away. She will not listen—will not hear it.

A week passes rapidly. Too rapidly for Rika. Each day only confirms her fears more as Bert coughs sometimes till his face is blue. Albert knows that Rika's fears are not imagination.

As the doctor examines little Bert, his expression betrays his deep concern. "Your little boy is very sick," he tells Rika. "He has pneumonia. Perhaps it's caused by—"

"Don't say it!" screams Rika.

"Calm yourself, Rika," rebukes Albert. "Babies can survive pneumonia."

The doctor busies himself with preparing some medicine. "Here," he says as he hands Rika a small bottle. "Try to give your baby a little of this. It will relieve his cough. There is nothing I can give him for the lung infection. He will have to fight that battle alone. You keep him warm and nurse him if he cares to do so. He is in God's hands. I can do no more."

Albert and Rika walk quietly out of the door. Albert's coughing is forgotten.

"Why didn't you let me take him to the doctor last week?" Rika asks angrily. "I knew he was very sick then."

Albert cannot respond. His whole body and soul are crying out in anguish while, at the same time, his lungs are screaming for a coughing spell that he is determined to suppress.

Rika lays little Bert in his small bed. Tears of anger and sorrow drop onto the blanket and onto his pallid face. Anger at Albert, anger at God, anger at herself. Tears of sorrow for the little life that hangs by a thread.

Albert drops dejectedly into a chair and tears come that he cannot restrain. His body convulses in sobs, then in coughing. Rika's feeling of love for him returns as she flies to his side.

"Oh, Albert, I'm so sorry I was angry. I didn't mean to hurt you. It isn't your fault that little Bert is sick."

She creeps onto his lap and they weep softly on each other's shoulders.

"We must tell Mama and Papa," says Albert.

"Yes, do," responds Rika. "Tell them to come, because I know little Bert is very sick."

Albert quickly disappears outside and runs the few blocks to his parents' home. They have been aware that the baby has been sick, but the seriousness of his illness has been withheld from them by Albert's assurances that it was only a cold.

Albert and the two grandparents are by the tiny crib in moments, but the short gasps and the bluish face tell them that death is near.

Death. No stranger to Rika. Yet, the thought of death for little Bert is unbearable. The final event overwhelms her. Even when Pastor Van Beck comes, his comforting words seem to fall on deaf ears. It is only when Herr DeLoof comes and envelops her with his arms that the pent-up tears are really released. He knows how hurt she is feeling, how angry she is and he understands. "Life must go on," he says as he leaves.

The shoe cobbler's shop and home are soon busy again with customers. Life is quieter for a time, but soon laughter again finds its way into the life of Albert and Rika.

"Guess what?" exclaims Rika at breakfast one morning, "I think we are going to have another baby."

Albert beams, "I've prayed for that every day since Bert died. We will really watch out so it won't catch a cold this time, won't we? Our sorrow has indeed turned into joy again."

"I wonder what God will give us this time, a boy or a girl?" ponders Rika.

"I'll be happy with either one," he replies. "Or maybe one of each?" he adds with a laugh. "My cousin has twins."

Days flow into months of expectancy and soon a daughter arrives. The death of little Bert is nearly forgotten in the happiness of new life in the Nykerk home.

"Annetje, that is a beautiful name," says Albert. "I like Anna for short, too."

"Let's always call her Annetje," objects Rika. "The name Anna hurts too much. I hope we can show Annetje to my mother. Maybe, just maybe, she will want to hold her. I would really love to see Mother do that."

"We will go to Amsterdam as soon as the baby is old enough to travel," agrees Albert. Then he adds, "The business is doing well, and I have begun to save some money for a home with a garden and flowers like you always talk about. I've been putting it in a box on the top shelf in the shop. It's behind a lot of stuff. Only our one employee knows where it is and he is a very honest person. I can trust him."

"How soon do you think we can buy a house?" Anna asks excitedly.

"At the rate we are saving now, we can maybe buy one in two years."

"I hardly dare to dream about it too much," says Rika. "I always think of Mama and Papa's dream and what happened to that."

"But we aren't dreaming about America," counters Albert. "I like Holland and I want to stay here."

"And I live wherever you live," Rika adds, as she places a warm kiss on his cheek.

Annetje is a happy baby and is the pride and joy of the Nykerk family.

Albert still has those coughing spells, but he has put on some weight and he goes for a walk every day to get exercise. Still, a persistent cough is a constant concern for Rika. She still wants him to go to the doctor, but he refuses. Annetje smiles and gurgles in her crib, but her every cough sends chills through Rika's body.

"Oh, God," she prays, "we asked for this child and we thank you for her. Please let us keep her."

Is it premonition or imagination? Rika is sure she hears the dreaded, familiar labored breathing as she bathes her precious daughter one morning.

"Albert!" she shouts. "Come here, right away. Annetje's breathing just like little Bert did at first!"

Albert turns pale as he watches and listens to the baby's breathing. Annetje turns her face to him and smiles.

"I really don't notice anything different," he says. "She seems to feel good, just look at her smile."

"I guess I'm so sensitive that I imagine things. But I surely was frightened for awhile."

"She is all right," he assures her. "We will watch her and if we see any signs of trouble, we'll take her to the doctor right away."

Three days later Rika's fears become a reality. Annetje is coughing and has a high fever. This time there is no disagreement about going to the doctor. The doctor tenderly examines Annetje. Albert and Rika watch his face anxiously. His frown and puzzled expression cause them to tremble with fear.

"Your daughter is quite sick," he tells them. "I hope we can help her. It's rather unusual, but she has some of the same symptoms that your little son had. I can't tell whether it is pneumonia or tuberculosis. Both are hard for babies, as you well know."

He turns to face them and says, "There is so little that we can do for small babies when they have trouble with their lungs."

"Is there no help?" Albert pleads.

"I can only give medicine. And you can keep her warm." He pauses. "Only God can heal her."

"You told us that when we brought Bert here," snaps Rika.

"Yes, I know. But it is still true. Maybe someday. . ."

"Is God going to let this baby die, too?" Rika asks angrily.

"I don't know, Rika. I don't know."

Albert and Rika go home with heavy hearts. Albert runs to his parents' home to share his concern while Rika holds Annetje tightly in her arms. After leaving his parents, he rushes home. Stepping hesitantly into the room, he asks numbly, "What do we do now?"

"I'm praying. But I feel like God isn't listening."

Albert sits on the edge of the bed in silence. Rika places Annetje in her crib and sits beside Albert and weeps. The pattern is so familiar. The hurts, the tears, the anger. Then the sorrow and the funeral. All are like a replay of Bert's death. Five months after her birth, Annetje is laid to rest in a grave beside Bert.

But life has to go on. Rika spends much of her time in the shop. Albert says little, but his cough is returning and the stress of the last months have caused him to lose weight again. Rika is concerned, but her sorrow has numbed her so much that she does not mention it to him.

"Dare we pray for another child?" asks Rika one evening.

"I have," Albert replies, "and I hope he sends us one even though we did lose our first two. I have no regrets that God gave us Bert and Annetje. Our lives are richer because of them. Remember? In the Bible Job lost all his children and he said 'The Lord gave and the Lord has taken away. Blessed be the name of the Lord.' Yes, I want God to give us another child."

Rika has mixed emotions. The hurt has been so deep. Three months later, she announces to Albert, "You will soon be a papa again."

"Good! I am really happy about that."

"I hope it's a boy," Rika says. "And we will name him Albert. How would you like that?"

"That will be great! Maybe he can take over my shoe shop."

"Not so fast," says Rika. "He or she isn't even born yet."

Again, the months pass quickly and Albert Junior is born in June. His lusty cry at birth seems to tell the world he plans to stay. What a joy he is. Rika and Albert are thankful for their answered prayers.

But God's testing and trials are not over. In spite of all their praying and their physical efforts, little Albert joins his brother and sister seven months after his birth.

Albert is crushed. His body becomes a skeleton as it convulses with almost constant coughing. When he agrees to see the doctor, Rika knows what the verdict will be. She has seen him spit up blood, but her numbed heart can hurt no more. The doctor tells Anna that Albert not only has tuberculosis, but he seems also to have lost his will to live. Rika wonders, too, why she should want to live.

Feeling somehow responsible for their future, she coaxes, "Come on, Albert, we are still young and can find enjoyment in life. I love you. I need you. We still have each other."

"Rika," he replies, "I may be only 30 years old, but I am an old man and I'm tired of living. I've fought this tuberculosis for years. It may be our children receive their death sentences from me. Why should I live on? Let me lie with them and rest."

They walk together to their home in the growing darkness of the evening. It seems to Rika that the sun has set forever behind them.

The next few weeks, Albert sits stolidly in the sun while it is there, eats what Rika prepares for him and sleeps when he isn't coughing.

Nick, the hired helper, keeps the shop open, but business begins to falter. The customers are no longer getting the intricate designs and work that they had grown to expect.

Rika's stubborn courage, which she had inherited from her father, comes to her aid again. She takes care of Albert by herself and learns to manage the shop. Albert's parents are frequent visitors, but Albert is so weak that no amount of encouragement can arouse him from his apathy.

One bright spot comes into Rika's life when Herr DeLoof and his wife, Hendrickje, pay her a visit. They are getting old and have retired from their work as caretakers of the orphanage. However, their love and concern for their "greater family" never ceases. Hennie's face still radiates the love of Christ into every life she touches. Rika seeks her advice often in the dark days of Albert's illness.

Albert's body hangs on to life persistently in spite of his weakened condition. There are times when he even speaks of the house they had planned to buy for their children. The deadly germs of tuberculosis relentlessly destroy his lungs, until one beautiful Sunday morning when he calls Rika to his bedside.

"I'm going home to my children and to my Lord. You have been a wonderful wife and I have loved you more than I can tell. I wish we could have had a long life together, but it is not to be. Our savings are in the box in the shop. You can sell the shop and pay the bills. Don't call my parents now. I want to spend these last few hours with you alone."

Rika cries. "You can't leave me. I need you! I love you!"

"You are a strong woman, Rika, and you will manage. I just know you will. Why don't you visit your aunts near Oldebrook after I'm gone? Maybe you can build a new life there."

"But I don't want to leave here," protests Rika. "I've nearly forgotten my relatives, and many of them have gone to America."

"Maybe you can realize your parents' dream and go to America. It is a wonderful land, I have been told."

"I shall never forget our life here together. We have had so many joys and so many tears all in such a short time."

"Yes, and we have much more joy awaiting us in heaven. I'm so tired. I want to be relieved of this weak and sick body."

Albert's breath now comes in gasps. He tries to sit up and to get more air. Rika holds him in her arms as his soul returns to God who gave it.

"Good-bye, my darling," she whispers as she lays his
lifeless body down on the bed.

Death has been such a frequent visitor to Rika that the
funeral has become almost routine. Yet, the death of Albert is
different. After the children's deaths she and Albert could
pick up the pieces together and start over.

Rika now realizes she is again alone. She has friends, but no
family, no close relatives that she knows, and she is still young.
She has to admit, her faith has faltered many times as death
stalked into her home so often. What should she do now? She
cannot stay in her home behind the cobbler shop.

Nick, who had always been so trusted by Albert, did come to
the funeral, but does not return to the shop the next day, so
Rika has to leave the shop closed. She must pay some of the
bills that have accumulated from the doctor and the funeral.

I will sell the shop and go to Oldebrook to visit my aunts as
Albert suggested, she figures. I can always return here if I
want to.

She rises and goes into the shop to get the box with their
savings. She knows where it was kept, but has never known
exactly how much money it contained. There have been times
when Albert had to take out some funds for the unusual
expenses that came up.

Rika finds a chair and moves the material on the shelf. She
reaches for the box. Her hand feels nothing.

Where can it be? Rika wonders with panic. Albert told me
many times where to find it. There wasn't any reason to move
it.

She is very puzzled. She searches every nook and corner of
the shop, but finds no trace of the cash box. The shop was
locked all the time of the funeral and afterwards. There is no
sign of a break-in, of anyone's searching through the
materials. She thinks perhaps that Albert might have said
something to his parents about the cash box.

I'll ask them in the morning, she decides.

The next morning, she walks to the Nykerk home and tells them about her search.

"Do you remember Albert saying anything about the cash box?" she asks them.

"Why, yes, I knew there was one," says Albert's father. "But I don't know where he kept it, or even what the box looks like. We'll come and help you look for it."

"When Nick comes back to work he may know something about it," volunteers Albert's mother.

"I never thought of him," muses Rika. "Even though he didn't show up yesterday, he could be there by now. I'll ask him."

The three walk back to the shop and try to enter the shop door but find it locked. Rika uses her key, wondering why Nick isn't at work.

"I asked him to stay on to help clean up and to complete the remaining orders and finish any repairs for the customers. I'll go to that room where he stays as soon as we find the cash box."

A thorough search of the shop and their home fails to produce the box.

Rika sets off immediately to Nick's rooming house to ask about the cash box and why he hadn't come to work. She knocks at the door and an old man opens it.

"Is Nick in his room?" she asks.

"Oh, no. He left yesterday morning," the old man informs them. "He paid his back rent up to date and told us he had found a better room to stay in."

"Gone!" Rika cries. "Not gone for good!"

"That's what he told us," he assures Rika.

Slowly the truth dawns on her. Nick has disappeared with all her savings. She runs back to her home in a trance.

"Nick has left town with all of our savings!" she shouts. "I never dreamed he would do that. What a fool we were to leave all that cash in the shop!"

"Let's call the police," suggests Albert's father.

"It won't do much good," says Rika. "I don't even know how much there was in the box. I can't prove a thing. He and the money are gone and I can't prove he took it even if I find him. People are so cruel. Now I have nothing but the little stuff in this shop and our furniture. We rented the shop and our home, so I will have to sell everything soon and move somewhere else. I can't even sell the name and the business, it has run down so. Oh, where will I go?"

"You may stay with us until you decide what you plan to do," says Albert's mother.

"Thank you. I think I'll do that until I sell my things," Rika says appreciatively.

As the shop itself is in a good location, Rika is able to sell the business after all, to a young cobbler, along with most of her furniture. He pays her promptly, making Rika free to go. But where?

She decides to go to her aunts and stops to visit her mother before leaving.

Anna is sitting in a chair staring out the window when Rika walks in. Rika notices the windows are barred and that the custodian locks the door behind her.

"Mama, I'm Rika, your daughter," Rika says gently. "Don't you know me?" Anna turns her face toward Rika, looks at her coldly and says nothing. She turns her head back to the window and resumes her staring. A frown forms on her face, then a half smile flickers, but still not a word.

"Mama, I'm going to Aunt Bertha and Aunt Aaltje in Oldebrook," she says more deliberately. "Don't you remember?"

"No!" Anna explodes and jumps off her chair. She runs into another room.

Never has Rika felt so alone. It seems as though now her mother has died, too.

Mechanically, she walks to the door and is let out into the

street. Mechanically, too, she buys her train ticket to Oldebrook, and just as mechanically she climbs into the train and
sits down. The train speeds past the same fields that she had
pointed out so excitedly to her parents some 20 years before.

Where has all the excitement of going to America gone?
Where are the pretty flowers? The love and laughter of parents
who loved her? It seems as though she has spent two lifetimes
already and she isn't yet 30 years old. The train jolts to a stop
and Rika steps out.

"Rika," says Aunt Bertha, "you've grown so much. But I
would have recognized you anywhere. Do come to our home.
You must tell us about your heartaches. We have heard some
about all your sorrows and we're so sorry."

"Yes," says Rika, "I left here with loving parents and a
beautiful dream. I found a beautiful husband and God gave us
three children. And now I have nothing left. Nothing left on
this earth. God is still with me, but sometimes he is so far
away. I have health and by God's grace, I *will* start a new life.
Somehow, somewhere."

"Stay with us as long as you wish. And visit your other
aunts and uncles. We all love you and will help you."

Life is difficult in this country town and it takes some
adjusting, but soon some of the joys and freedom of country
living bring back pleasant memories of Rika's childhood.
However, to find work is difficult. There are very few homes
of wealth and consequently not much demand for maids.

Rika has thought that she would find it difficult to marry
again, but with the passing of time and making new friends in
these new surroundings, her life takes on renewed vigor. Her
experiences with sorrow and her natural-born determination to
make the best of whatever life holds out to her soon overcome
her grief. When a young man named Gerhart Fikse asks her to
be his wife, she accepts.

Gerhart is a day laborer like Rika's father had been and life is difficult. Wages are low, so they can afford only the cheapest food.

Within a year a son is born and they name him Chris in honor of Rika's father. He is a healthy baby, but he doesn't grow very fast. Rika realizes it is probably due to the poor diet he is getting. Still, she is sensitive to every cough and cold that little Chris has. Fortunately, he quickly recovers and is walking by the time he is a year old.

When little Chris is a year and a half old, he is joined by a brother, Bert. To get enough food to feed four mouths is now nearly impossible on the wages of a day laborer. Rika begins to dream the dream of her parents.

"Gerhart," she asks her husband, "do you think we could go to America?"

"Go to America!" he exclaims. "How? We don't have money enough to buy food. Where can we get enough to go to America? Forget it!"

"I think," persists Rika, "if I write Uncle Bert in America, he might loan us enough money to get there. Then we could pay him back by working for him or for someone else. There is plenty of food there. Maybe we can even have a farm and home of our own. I will write him tonight."

"Go ahead, it can do no harm. But I don't care much about the idea."

The letter is sent. Uncle Bert has already heard about the sorrow and struggles Rika has had and decides he will help her and Gerhart and their little family to get to America.

Six weeks later, Rika's hands shake as she reads this letter to Gerhart:

> Dear Rika and Gerhart,
>   I will send you the money to come and I'll guarantee that you will never be hungry again. America does not give food to people, but it will offer you a good life if you are willing to work. I know that you can and will do that, so your uncles

and other relatives here will be happy to help. Come to us and God's blessing to you.

Write us when you can come and I will send you the money. Be sure to get your tickets from a man you can trust. May God give you a good trip.

Greetings,
Uncle Bert

"I hate to leave my friends here," says Gerhart, "but we must have more food. We must go where we can get it. We'll go as soon as possible."

Rika can hardly believe it. The dream of her parents coming true? If only her mother, Anna, could know and understand that God was making Chris and Anna's dream come true through her children and grandchildren. The trip across the ocean is rough and the two little ones are sick most of the time. But what a joy to see the land of their dreams! The train ride seems to last forever. It is such a huge land!

"Oh, yes, there must be room for us!" cries Rika as she looks at the hundreds of miles of country speeding by the train window.

Rika lives to see more children grow strong and healthy. She lives to see the day when Gerhart and she own a large home and a large farm.

Now, as we trade our wooden shoes back again for some made of leather—or synthetics, perhaps—how can we forget the awesome footprints made by our relatives and friends of the past? I can't help feeling that, if Rika could have been here telling her story in person, she might have quoted this Bible verse in closing:

"The Lord is good unto them that wait on Him."

Lamentations 3:55

Part II

We Make a Start

1

Background

My grandpa, Hendrick Jan Schut, was born in Gelderland, Holland, in the year 1839. He died in July of 1900. Grandpa Schut married Allie Van den Berg, who was born in Holland, January 27, 1844. They were married there and had one child before they emigrated to America in 1866.. They got to Michigan in October of that year. They settled in the Alto, Wisconsin, area, staying there for only a few years, then moved to Newkirk, Iowa. Grandma Schut had ataxia and died about 1885.

There were nine children born to this marriage: Allie Schut (Klomp), Hattie Schut (Hendricks) (De Motts), Gerrit Jan, Carrie Schut (De Kraai), John, Nellie Schut (Tubergen), William, Henry, and Grace Schut (Eernissee).

Grandma Schut was buried in the Orange City Cemetery in Orange City, Iowa. After her death, my grandfather married Hendrikje Klein, a widow with four children (I do not know her maiden name). She was buried in Newkirk, Iowa, alongside Grandpa Schut. Their births and deaths can be verified on the gravestones there.

The inscription on Grandfather Schut's gravestone reads:

Hendrick Jan Schut
geb. Jan 30-1839
gestorven Jul. 23-1900

lk legt heir te rusten in het stof

51

Ik weet mijn heiland die komt weder
Die voert mij in het hemelhof
Ik ligt hier maar zoo lang ter neder
Te slaapen in het stille graf
Hij kompt. Ik legt daar dan mijn dood
kleed af.

Translated into English it means:
I lie here resting in the dust
I know my Savior comes again
He will transport me to heaven
I lie here, meanwhile, down
To sleep in the quiet grave.
He comes, I'll (then) take my death clothes off.

My Grandpa Mol was born in Gelderland, Nederland (the Netherlands), near Oldebroek village on January 5, 1859. He went A.W.O.L. from the army, and sailed for America at the age of 22.

My Grandma Mol (Bakker) was born in Oldebroek, Nederland. She emigrated to America when she was seven years old. Grandma and Grandpa both landed in the Pella, Iowa, area. Grandma Mol and her parents had been in America for some years before Grandpa Mol met Grandma in Pella. They were married February 14, 1883, somewhere in that area. Grandma Mol had very little schooling, but she was intelligent. All of my grandparents came from a peasant class in Holland and came to America practically penniless.

Grandpa Schut was a self-educated man and above average in intelligence. He and Grandpa Mol were both good managers, so after farming in America for 30 years both grandparents became relatively wealthy, though not rich. Grandpa and Grandma Mol had seven children: Jennie Mol (Schut), Artie Mol (Schut), Bertha Mol (Schut), Annie Mol (Plaggerman), Winnie Mol (Vandergon), Dr. Henry L. Mol,

and Johanna Mol (Graves) (Grogh). John Schut and Jennie
Mol were my father and mother. John Schut was born
February 6, 1877, and Jennie Mol, November 3, 1883. They
were married on February 14, 1908—on Valentine's Day, as
Grandpa and Grandma Mol had been 25 years before.

Grandpa Mol farmed around the Pella, Iowa, area for about
eight years after his marriage. Then, with his brother Chris,
who had married a sister of my Grandma Mol, they moved to
Sibly, Iowa. Together they operated a farm of 640 acres,
which was considered a very large farm in those days. They
farmed together with several hired men for 10 years. At the
end of that time they dissolved the partnership and each
bought a farm near Maple Lake, Minnesota. Grandpa Mol
bought a 160-acre farm on the east shore of Millstone Lake,
where the Zylstras live now. Chris bought a 130-acre farm on
the south shore of Sugar Lake, where his grandson, Cliff Mol,
now lives. They moved to their new farms in 1903.

My mother, Jennie Mol, was quite unhappy about the move.
She was 20 years old and could not see how anyone could
make a living on such a small farm. However, she adjusted
quite well because she did not have to do as much farm work
there. Being the oldest in a succession of five girls, my mother
had been Grandpa Mol's right hand and had to milk and do
chores as well as field work. She often remarked that picking
corn by hand had been the most difficult work for her. They
had to hook up the horses to the wagon in the morning before
it was light, go to the field with a kerosene lantern and find the
first row that hadn't been picked. As soon as it was light, they
would begin. The mornings were, at times, frosty. I remember
her telling us how she had cried because of her cold hands.
But, as Grandpa Mol was from the "old school," he believed
the husband and father to be the absolute ruler of the
household. He also expected obedience and hard work from
his hired hands, but he paid them well. He was the boss and no
one questioned his position. Because of his strong views on

Christianity and his administrative ability, he served on several
church boards. He was known to be firm, but fair and honest.
He had an unusual physical appearance. His full beard and
full head of hair had turned pure white at an early age, so he
was often referred to as "*de witte Mol*" which translated
means "the white mole."

Grandma Mol was a timid, meek person. Whether she was
that way by nature, or became that way because of her
husband, I do not know. She suffered a great deal from
migraine headaches and died in 1924 when she was in her
early 60s.

Grandpa Mol was highly respected by his children and the
community in spite of his sometimes stern discipline and
manner. He had a tremendous sense of humor and loved to
travel, which he did extensively. He returned to Holland twice,
and after Grandma died he took his Model T and traveled
through South Dakota, Nebraska and Iowa to visit all the
relatives. He had been able to retire at 56 and lived a rich,
eventful life. He died in 1939 from cancer of the prostate
when he was 80 years old.

My father, John Schut, lived his life in Sioux County, Iowa.
He was a very strong man and spent every fall working on a
threshing crew. He had a great knowledge of how a threshing
machine operated and was hired as manager of the machine.

I know very little of his young life. He seldom spoke about
it. Besides, I was only 14 years old when he died, so we had
very few years in which we could share experiences on an
adult level. I do know he loved to sing, and that he sang in the
youth choir. He had a short temper, but quickly forgot his
anger. He had not yet made confession of his faith in Jesus
Christ when he was married. That was in 1908 when he was 31
years old. He thought it was presumptuous to make a
statement that anyone could be a child of God. He believed
God was sovereign and saved only those whom He
willed—and my father wasn't sure that it was God's will to

save him. However, after one year of marriage he did become a confessing member of the church.

He was very sensitive to any remarks about his person. He had one blind eye and his teeth were crooked, so he felt somewhat inferior. We were strictly forbidden to call him "Daddy" or "Dad." Those titles were considered disrespectful.

My parents, whom I shall call Mom and Pa for the rest of this book, were well fitted for each other. The one was the complement of the other. They were, in a real sense, one. While Pa was impatient, moody and hot tempered, Mom was patient, kind and seldom became angry. She always looked at life with enthusiasm and nothing seemed to get her down.

Pa considered the Holland language superior to English, especially in expressing spiritual truths. He taught us how to read the Bible in the Holland language. I learned the alphabet while sitting on his lap as he held the Old Dutch Bible.

That brings to mind a custom Pa always practiced in our home. He had us pray silently before and after each meal, and he read a chapter from the Bible after each meal. It was an extremely rare occasion that he missed, although there were times during the rush season that he would turn to a short Psalm instead of a long chapter of the history of the Israelites. I recall, too, how at times there were long lists of names which he would skip over. Nevertheless, the Bible would be completely read by the end of the year and we would start again from the beginning.

Mom often told us of a rather humorous "ceremony" that took place when she was a young girl in Iowa. She said the hired men would take a handful of milk and baptize each calf and give it a biblical name. They used a short Dutch verse that said the milk running over the calf's head would signify baptism. Consequently, their calves had names such as Habbakuk, Nehemiah, Esther and others of that nature. I have never seen that done.

Perhaps one of the greatest changes through the years has come about in attitudes toward human behavior. Preparation for the observances of Sunday used to begin the day before.

All possible cooking for the Sunday meals was done on Saturday. Likewise, the clothes to be worn on Sunday were carefully laid out, kerosene lamps were filled and trimmed and the floors were cleaned. Extra wood for the stove was brought into the kitchen and extra water for home use was carried in from the pump. Every effort was made to make Sunday quiet and restful. The barn was cleaned out late Saturday and extra hay was thrown down from the loft to be fed quickly to the livestock the following morning. The cream separator was usually washed daily, but on Sunday we only ran clean hot water through the machine. Our cream was never delivered to the creamery on Sunday. It was kept in cold water until Monday. We were not allowed to play ball, horseshoe or any other game of exertion on Sundays. This rule was difficult to enforce with four active boys around. We usually found things to take their place that were at least as energetic. We could never attend any doings on the Lord's day except a church function. Once when Bert and I spent an hour walking through the woods, Pa gave us a good lecture on the sins of walking unnecessarily on Sunday.

Divorce was practically unheard of and a girl with an illegitimate child was labeled for life. Premarital sex was uncommon and any reference to it was kept within the bounds of those who practiced it. The subject of sex was never discussed between young people and adults, and seldom between parents and children. These conditions may have been different in other areas and families, but I'm recording only what I observed in the small community where I lived. I don't plan to make any judgments on the morals and customs of those times or on those that I observe today. The openness and freedom with which sex is discussed today, in contrast to fifty years ago, makes it difficult to compare the rightness or wrongness of methods and customs of the two eras. Sin in every form has been present since creation. It can be conquered by faith in Christ and His redeeming love and forgiveness. That remains the same.

Petty problems, disagreements and long-time feuds between families, as well as within them, were more common. However, relationships were seldom permanently broken. Perhaps the mobility of today's society has lessened friction. If you can't get along with someone, you can always move. That wasn't so easy in the early 1900s.

Today's children would wonder at the comparative ignorance of my generation concerning how the rest of the world lived. I recall receiving a letter from a cousin in Florida who told about walking barefooted in January. I couldn't believe it. I know Mom stared in utter disbelief when she heard about homosexuals living in the cities.

2

Changing Customs

In chapters to come, I tell of some dramatic and rapid changes that have come about in farming, homemaking, transportation, eating, education and many other areas of life. Of equal importance are the subtle and sometimes imperceptible ways that our thinking, life style, value system, social mores and spiritual beliefs were affected by all these outward changes.

In this chapter, I hope to relate how society and my own philosophies have changed. I hope to be able to do this without passing judgment on either the past or the present practices. That won't be easy.

Not long ago, a father of a teenage son asked a grandfather, "What did you do when your father asked you to do something?"

"We did it. And now!" was the prompt reply.

"You mean to say, you never argued?"

"We *never* argued with Pa when we were told to do something. We knew better."

"What do you mean by that?"

"We knew that any challenge to Pa's command would be met with alternative commands or actions that would be far worse."

"But how do you enforce a command with a teenager?" asked the father in exasperation.

"You start when they are in the crib, when you *can* enforce your request or command. It's too late when they are 10 or older," said the grandfather.

"With this talk about children's rights, some forget that parents also have rights," he continued. "Not only that, it's a parent's God-ordained responsibility to expect obedience and respect from his child."

"But, doesn't a child have a right to voice his objection to an unreasonable demand?" countered the father.

Grandfather thought for a moment. "Who decides what is unreasonable? I know I thought Pa was very unreasonable at times. Even today I think there were times when Pa recognized his demands were harsh and he changed them. But he was always the judge of what was unreasonable and what was not."

"It wouldn't work today!" insisted the father.

"Perhaps not, but we had much more love and respect for our father than I see children having for their parents today. I want to stress the word respect. Because, without *respect*, a parent also the loses the child's love."

"Things sure are different today," concluded the father.

The concept that the father and husband carried the absolute authority in the home was part of the culture and custom that emigrated with the early settlers from Europe and it took several generations before a change could be perceived.

It was the parents, not the school law, that decided if and when a child went to school and when they were to quit school. Very few children went to high school; higher education was considered unnecessary for the operation of a farm and most boys were expected to become farmers.

The minister of our small church was held in high esteem and no one called him or his wife by their first names. Women had no voice in church government until some time in the 1920s. They were permitted to teach Sunday School classes, but only a minister or elder was permitted to teach catechism classes.

As a young man I once called an older man by his first name. He reported it to my mother and she asked me about it.

"Yes," I said, "I guess I did, but I don't see why that is so wrong."

"You don't call anyone who is as old as your father or older by his first name unless they ask you to do so," was her firm reply.

Also, I think the average person of today has a different concept of God than 60 years ago. Our parents and grandparents spoke of God who was angry with mankind. Any trouble, trial or tragedy was to be accepted without question.

Also, a commitment made to God or sanctioned by Him was expected to remain unbroken under all or any circumstances. The marriage vow was one of these and a divorced person found it difficult to be accepted into the church. Pledges and promises were expected to be kept. Not that this always happened, but there was considerable social pressure to do so.

The decision of the parent, police, pastor, priest or teacher was absolute. With this type of philosophy, society was more stable. Changes came slowly.

The concept of a loving, caring God was not stressed in those days. That God would take a personal interest in all the problems people face was inconceivable. To speak and sing to God in a nonchalant or personal manner was considered to be disrespectful.

In today's society and in the church, we tend to speak more personally and openly, as though God were a friend. We tend to think He overlooks our weaknesses and is not concerned about a broken promise or commitment. Today we find friends willing to share some of their innermost feelings and thoughts with each other, too. God seems much more real. More intimate.

The many different beliefs that people have are also due to a tremendous increase in our tolerating the views and opinions of others. The increase in education and contacts with people of different views helps us to determine the worth of ideas and old values and to change our ideas for better and sometimes for worse.

The stress, danger and discomfort of hooking up a team of horses to a bobsled to go four miles to a New Year's Eve church service when the temperature was 20 below zero Fahrenheit was something to contend with. Today, all that has been replaced by the strain and stress of time scheduling a family where the parents and children all want to go to different places at different times for different reasons.

I have to note, too, how family birthday parties, once so important, have been replaced by sports activities, school parties, and other social events.

The tolerance of another person's beliefs and ideas has certainly helped to promote better interpersonal relationships. The time when parents disowned their son or daughter if they married a member of another church is nearly past. The suspicion (and often hatred) between churches of different denominations is mostly gone. Perhaps some of the good that has come from this change is offset by the Christian's acceptance of life styles and beliefs that bear very little resemblance to the firm convictions of earlier generations.

How do I feel about this? I have mixed emotions. I am grateful that I have learned to love and respect people with different Christian beliefs.

I am grateful that I have learned to love the sinner in spite of his wicked ways and that I can accept him or her without condoning the behavior.

I am grateful, too, for parents and grandparents who were uncompromising in their commitments to God, to children and to their spouses.

I am grateful for friends who support and confirm my better behavior and accept me in spite of my faults.

I cherish the memory of parents who had a childlike faith and who instilled in me certain absolutes that have sustained me in times of temptation.

The change I mentioned earlier, from a predominantly male-dominated society to a shared responsibility of tasks and

authority, has happened mostly during my lifetime. In my
early years (remember, I was born in 1910) the roles of a man
and woman were quite clearly defined in the home, business
and in society. The wife was given authority by the husband to
make decisions in only clearly defined areas. Permission was
needed for her to make decisions not delegated by the man.
Many husbands, however, felt they were destined to do as they
pleased and the wives were lucky if they were even told about
an upcoming decision until it had been made.

In this time of "woman's lib," it is difficult to understand
how a woman could be happy under such restrictions. Yet, I
am certain that my mother and aunts were happier than many
women today who are free from total male domination.

There were, perhaps, various reasons why this was so. I
expect the most obvious one was the training and expectations
that were a part of their home environment. The term
"brainwashed" was not part of our language at that time, but
it does define how girls and boys were expected and educated
to fulfill their respective roles in society and in the family
structure. This standard was, of course, not accepted by all
women. There were some families where the authority and
decision making were shared, or in some cases, reversed.

Much of the rationale for a male-dominated family and
society came from the belief that man was destined by God to
fulfill the role of the head of the home and women were
destined to be subject to men in all things. The man was
considered the priest in his home and was supposed to lead the
family in all spiritual matters. In my parents' and
grandparents' home, the husband led in prayer, read the Bible
aloud and checked the children's knowledge of their
catechism lessons. When my father died, my mother assumed
all these duties, indicating that she was capable of doing so.

I do not remember ever seeing my father or any of my
uncles washing dishes, baking, doing laundry or changing
diapers. If they did, I'm sure they would have made sure no
other man saw them. To be caught would have brought an

accusation that they had capitulated to the wife (a never-to-be-forgotten error). As a young boy, I do recall seeing a husband peeling potatoes for his wife and I thought that was quite unusual.

The dating game was played by a different set of rules—or perhaps we should say by a more subtle application of the same rules that are used today. Girls seldom asked for dates, but there were many ways of communicating without using words. The results were usually the same.

It was not uncommon to have the girl's father come to the car within 15 minutes after the couple's return to the girl's home. The father's voice was always firm and left no room for discussion.

"You may come and visit with my daughter in the house, but not out here in the car." The invitation was usually accepted, but you can be sure the young man was home early!

Rules varied greatly from parent to parent and from community to community. Some parents had few restrictions on their children, but they were in the minority in the church group in which I grew up.

Prohibition (the eighteenth amendment to the U.S. Constitution which was against any intoxicating beverages) was in effect during the years I was ages nine through twenty-three. My parents did have some whiskey in our home before prohibition became law. They had used it sometimes for medicine and I remember a few times that my father took a swallow when the weather was hot. However, when prohibition became the law of the land, we had no alcohol in our home, nor did Father ever use it.

"Home brew" (beer) and wine were made in many homes and homemade stills produced "moonshine" (whiskey) by the gallon. The illicit product had no labels and there was no way to determine its alcoholic content. It wasn't possible to know what the moonshine had been made from, nor just how clean the machinery was in which it had been made. Nearly everybody except the prohibition officers knew how to obtain it. Even though I knew where and how to get moonshine, I never dared to drink it.

Prohibition was considered a failure. Personally, I think the intent of the law was good, but it lacked the support of the majority of the people. I know it did dry up a few heavy drinkers and a drunk usually kept out of sight, or was kept under cover by his friends until he was sober.

Smoking by young boys generally started with dried corn silk or some Prince Albert tobacco "borrowed" from their father's tobacco can. It was rolled in ordinary white paper and the guy who coughed and sputtered the least was considered the most mature of the group. We never heard of marijuana, or I expect some would have tried that, too.

The ultimate on the road to adulthood was to smoke one of Dad's cigars. The first one was seldom smoked in its entirety. Usually, about halfway, the boy's face would become grayish green and any meal he may have had in the preceding two or three hours was "discarded."

3

Horses Make Way for Autos

Transportation and travel have probably undergone their greatest changes during my lifetime. The railroad train had made quite an impact on traveling over long distances before I was born, but private transportation was still done mostly by horse, using the buggy in the summer and the sled in the winter. The transition from horse and buggy to automobile was slow at first, because public roads were not built to accommodate autos. Besides, the first autos were relatively expensive and not very dependable. An automobile tire, for instance, seldom lasted more than two or three thousand miles. I can recall vividly an advertisement for a tire claiming that it would travel five thousand miles. My father said, "I don't believe it."

There were times that a car would stall for no apparent reason, forcing the occupants either to walk home or ask the nearest neighbor for a ride.

My parents bought their first car in 1915. It was an Overland touring car. I recall that the dealer made an offer to my father. Pa said he didn't have a garage for it, but if the dealer would build one for him, Pa would buy it. To his surprise, the car dealer took him at his word and built a corrugated steel garage for the car. Pa kept his promise and he bought the car. It proved to be a lemon. Four years later we traded it for a new 1919 four-cylinder touring Studebaker. The touring adjective meant that the fabric roof or top would fold back and all would be open to the sun—and rain.

The top, of course, could be put up again and side curtains fastened with clips to the top and body to protect us from the weather. There were no heaters, but it didn't really matter. There was no antifreeze on the market, either. As soon as winter set in, each wheel was raised from the ground and blocked up to keep the strain off the tires. The battery was removed and stored in the cellar, and the auto had a rest until the next spring.

Many of the concepts of the automobile engine were not understood. I remember one time when the starter wouldn't go and we had a mechanic come out. He told us that the battery was discharged and dead. "You don't run it enough to keep the battery charged up," he said.

"You mean to tell us that the more we run it, the better the battery will work?" Mom asked.

"Yes," he said. "The generator puts energy that you have used to start the car back into the battery while it is running. If you use the starter too often and don't run the car, the battery will finally go dead."

Mom looked at him with disbelief in her eyes, but didn't reply. Later she said to Pa, "That doesn't make sense, the more you use a battery, the better it works."

Her idea was that using anything caused it to wear out, and in most cases she was right. The idea that a battery could be regenerated by running the car was truly a foreign concept to her.

The top speed of our Studebaker was perhaps around 35 mph, but we seldom exceeded 20 mph, because of Mom. She would see the trees and fence posts fly by and caution, "*Niet zoo hart! Niet zoo hart!*" Translated from the Holland, she meant, "Not so fast! Not so fast!"

My grandfather Mol would tell Mom, "Don't look at the trees and fence posts close to the car. Look way ahead and you won't notice how fast you are going."

The roads were still made for buggies and wagons, not for

speeding or passing. It was common practice to sound the horn around every corner to warn any approaching vehicle that the center of the road was occupied and that each vehicle should prepare to veer to the right as far as possible.

Not all horses appreciated the new contraptions coming down the road. We had a horse named Frank who had a hearty disdain for them. We always had to drive out of the road as far as we could if he happened to be harnessed up on the left side because he would inevitably let go at the auto with one hind foot. Several cars received the imprint of his hard hoof before Pa made sure there was enough room between him and a car.

Any rain or snow meant that the car got a rest and the horses were pressed into service again. We had a two-seated buggy (or surrey) with a fabric top. It even had side curtains to protect those in the back seat. I remember, as spring came and the roads dried up, the horses would move along at a brisk trot. Then Pa would say, "In a few weeks we can get the auto going and the horses can rest on Sunday while we go to church."

Getting to and from school didn't pose much of a problem. That depended on our two sturdy legs and a half-hour of time. We lived about a mile and a half from the school if we followed the road, or about one mile if we cut across the fields and pastures. On rare occasions, when there was a severe snowstorm, Pa or one of the neighbors would come after us. If it was stormy in the morning, we stayed home. During the winter, when the snow was deep, we and the neighboring Hoekstra children would walk single file across the fields with the oldest one breaking the way. Eventually, this path to school became well packed.

Some of the children had skis that they used when the snow was very deep. Because we could not afford to buy any, Pa bought two pine boards and made points on them. To get the points turned up so they would skim over the snow, we soaked those ends in a boiler of boiling water for several hours to soften them up. Then by putting the points between two planks nailed onto a frame, we could bend the points to the desired curve. They had to dry for several days. We nailed leather straps in a loop at the center of each ski into which we could place the toe of our overshoes.

We had only one pair of these, so when my brother Bert and I both went to school we had to take turns using them while the other one walked. The skis served us for recreation during the long noon hour. We used them to slide down the hills near our school. Quite frequently, Bert and I would each take one ski and go down the hill with one foot placed in front of the other. It took a keen sense of balance and there were many tumbles. That was preferable to taking turns, which meant waiting on top of the hill until the other had walked back up. We'd never heard of a ski lift. We made ski jumps of snow which made us sail through the air for a short way, but we usually landed with our seats in the snow, the skis going down the hill without us. These were not skis with heel straps, just with straps over the toes. That meant we lost our skis every time we tumbled, unless someone coming up the hill would catch them for us.

One day in early September (1919 or 1920), shortly after we had purchased our 1919 Studebaker, Pa, Ma, Bert, my sister Elsie and I took a trip to Chandler, Minnesota, a distance of two hundred miles. We started at 5 a.m. and arrived at 7 p.m. after a hot and dusty trip. There wasn't a single mile paved.

Roads had no numbers. The roads were designated as the "green and white trail" or the "yellow and black trail" and so on. At intersections some telephone poles or fence posts had green and white stripes on them with an "R" painted on the white portion if the trail made a right turn or an "L" if it turned to the left. I don't recall any stop signs anywhere, as traffic was very light and slow. There were many hills where we had to shift down to medium or low gear to make it to the top. The term "second" was not used. The Model T Fords had only two forward speeds.

We owned Model Ts at various times. The stories and feats of these versatile autos could fill a book. Ma bought our first Model T some years after Pa died. It was a 1924 model and I was about 18 or 19 years old. It had a spotlight on it which was wired to the magneto. When the motor was running it produced a very bright light that we could turn and focus on any object we wished. We took particular delight in shining our so-called searchlight on the windows of homes as we passed by. The Schut boys' reputation didn't improve any with this bright light being focused suddenly on a darkened window.

We had cut off the back seat of that Model T and fastened a wooden box on it like a pick-up truck. Since the box was a little long for that short wheelbase, the front end would rise up when we put on too heavy a load, as we frequently did. Then we couldn't steer.

On one occasion, Bert and I decided to deliver five large hogs to the stockyards in Maple Lake. All went well until we tried to climb a steep hill near town. The Ford could not make it in high, so I shifted into low. The front end came up and I couldn't steer. We swung crosswise on the road and were headed for the side. As I let up on the low gear, the front end came down with a jolt. I maneuvered the truck back parallel to the road, but any attempt to climb the hill resulted in the same problem.

Bert jumped out and said, "I'll hang onto the front end. Maybe my weight will keep the front end down." But he could not counterbalance those five hogs. What to do?

I don't recall who got the idea, but we decided the front end might stay down if we turned the truck around and backed it up the hill. The hogs should then move to the front. We managed to turn the truck around, and it worked! We backed to the top of the hill and into a driveway, then went forward the rest of the way to Maple Lake. We had to do this on many future occasions.

During this time we also owned a 1927 Chevrolet sedan. It was used for passenger transportation. At times, the old Model T would not start. It didn't have a battery or starter, and its "spark" for the spark plugs was generated by a magneto. This was sometimes short-circuited by a piece of dirt. To take care of this, we would drive the Chevrolet alongside the Ford and wire the battery of the Chevrolet to the magneto of the Ford. With a jack holding up the hind wheel of the Ford, and the gears in high, that wheel would act as a flywheel to maintain the momentum of the motor—if it started. We would then crank the Ford by giving the crank a quick half-turn up and then letting go. There was a good reason for letting go. Only one wire was used from the battery to the magneto. The connection was completed by pushing the door of the Chev against the body of the Ford. The result was that when the Ford started, the high voltage of its magneto made both cars "hot" and gave anyone a good jolt if they touched either one. To break the circuit and cut off the high voltage, we would then take a pitchfork and close the door of the Chevrolet. After getting it started, we usually had no trouble until it shorted out again.

One of the first autos to have glass windows on the doors and rear panel was the Essex. Our neighbors, the Dykhuizens, bought one in 1923 or 1924. They frequently took Mom along to church. As she told it, she "sat in a glass case" while she went to church. It was a marvel to her.

The most memorable events that I experienced with the Model T Ford were associated with a 1924 coupe. It was owned by a cousin of mine, Joe Eernissee. In August 1933, Bert W. Schut (another cousin of mine) and I rode with him to his home in Timber Lake, South Dakota, to visit his family. His mother, Grace, was my father's sister.

Coming home, we crossed the northern border into

Westfield, North Dakota, where we picked up a passenger who was going to Central College in Pella, Iowa, where my cousins were enrolled and I planned to enter in September. To accommodate him, we took off the trunk and fixed an open air "rumble seat" in the trunk where two of us could ride. We left Westfield in the evening and drove straight through, arriving back home at 11 a.m. What a ride!

That winter, after being home for the Christmas-New Year's holiday, that coupe was again packed with cousins and bound for Central College. I was a freshman; Jim Schut, a sophomore; Joe Eernissee, a junior, and Harold Schut, a senior.

That night was bitter cold! Somewhere below zero. We took turns sitting on each other's laps both for comfort and for warmth. It was midnight when we started from Minneapolis, and 3 a.m. when we arrived in Faribault, Minnesota. I was sitting on Jim's lap when he said, "We have to stop! I think my toes are frozen!" He could hardly walk, but he made it into a cafe that was open. The chili beans we had there were perhaps the best I've ever tasted before or since.

After warming up there, we resumed our trip. The car had a hot manifold heater in it, but it was so cold out that it was still difficult to stay warm. As we got farther south and the morning sun came out, we were able to get warm again. We stopped in Grundy Center, Iowa, where my uncle, Dr. Henry Mol, lived. He gave us a good meal at a local cafe and we started out again for Pella and Central College. That was about 3 p.m. We were rolling merrily along when suddenly the right rear wheel came off and rolled past us. We came to a very abrupt halt as the side of the rear end slid on the gravel road. A cloud of dust arose into the air and small rocks sailed into the roadside ditch. The wheel continued rolling for several hundred feet as Harold shouted after it, "Hey, wait for us!"

A quick inspection revealed that the five bolts used to hold the wheel on the brake drum and axle had sheared off. We had no bolts to replace them, so I hitchhiked the eight miles back to Grundy Center and purchased five new ones for 25 cents. Rather than hitching another ride, I went to my uncle and explained our predicament. He was very amused and laughed heartily, but immediately took his car and drove me back to Joe's coupe. In a matter of minutes, we had replaced the wheel and were on our way again. But our troubles were not over.

As we were all very short on cash and thought we could make it to Pella, we had chosen not to buy any more gas. We hadn't reckoned on the steep hills north of town, nor on one of the peculiarities of every Model T Ford. The gas tank was under the front seat and the gas fed into the carburetor by gravity. This caused no problem as long as the tank was at least one-fourth full, or while traveling on a level road. In climbing a long hill with the gas tank nearly empty, however, the fuel could not run into the carburetor. As soon as the small supply in the carburetor was exhausted, the motor would stop. About six miles north of Pella it happened. We were nearly to the town and the motor stopped. We got out to survey the situation and decided that by turning around and backing up the hill, the tank would be higher than the carburetor so the gas could run into it. This worked out well and we backed up two more hills, but there was one long hill left. It was about four miles before Pella. The extra effort of turning around and going backwards up those hills had completely exhausted our gas supply. It was now 11 p.m. The farm homes were mostly dark. We knocked at the door of one nearby and asked the farmer if he had any gas he could sell us. He said, "I'm sorry, but I don't."

When we told him about our troubles, he was very helpful. He suggested, "If you have a Model T and there is just a little gas left to get the motor started, it will continue to run on kerosene. I can give you a couple gallons of that."

It seemed worth a try. We shook the car a bit to get the last of the gas into the carburetor. Whoopee! It started!

We quickly poured in the kerosene and it did continue to run just as the farmer had said. We paid and thanked him and went on our way again. We had gone only a mile when the kerosene fumes became so strong inside the car that we could hardly breathe. We stopped again and decided that three of us would stand on the running boards and Joe Eernissee could drive. (In case you're too young to remember, a running board was a narrow eight-inch steel step connecting the front and rear fenders.) We opened both windows and kept directing the fresh outside air into the car so Joe could breathe. We drove the remaining three miles into Pella like that, arriving there at 1 a.m. Fortunately, the weather there was much warmer than when we had started from Minneapolis 25 hours earlier. That was really a trip to be remembered.

The old Model T truck we had on the farm was used for many things. When our one-cylinder gas engine wore out, we could not afford to buy another. That made it difficult for Mom, as the engine had been used to run the washing machine and to pump water when there wasn't enough wind to turn the windmill. Then we used the Ford's motor by backing the truck up to the windmill, bolting a small pulley onto one hind wheel, then jacking that wheel up and adding a pulley made from an old automobile tire to run the water pump.

We used the same sort of hook-up, when necessary, to run the washing machine that was kept out on the porch. It was all a rather makeshift affair, but the old Ford motor idled along easily and it worked out quite well. It used more gas than the other engine, but gas was cheap, only 13 or 15 cents per gallon.

The old Model T Ford was perhaps the simplest automobile ever built. We often said, "If you have a plier, a screwdriver and a piece of wire with you, you could always fix any problem well enough to get home."

Through no fault of its own, the old truck nearly caused us a

dreadful tragedy. One winter afternoon when I was home
from college for the holidays, several of us Schut cousins went
over to Indian Lake, about a mile west of our home, to skate.
There was constant urging to take the truck onto the ice and
make it spin around and around. I wasn't so sure the ice was
thick enough to hold the weight, so I wasn't too enthused. The
others assured me that it was safe, and I started the truck.
About six of the boys jumped into the box in back. Maybe
two hundred feet out, I noticed the ice waving ahead of me.

"Everybody get off!" I yelled.

They didn't need any persuading. They had seen it too. I
couldn't turn short enough on the smooth ice to get back to
where we had driven onto the lake, but by making a long slow
arch I reached the shore nearly a quarter of a mile away. The
water was swishing up from under the ice as I drove onto the
shore. I often think back to how close we were to a horrible
tragedy. All seven of us would have drowned if we had broken
through. There was over 40 feet of water under that ice. Our
guardian angel must have been present at that moment. For
that matter, I think we all kept the angel quite busy when we
were young.

In the early days of autos, they were never considered for
transportation in winter or when roads were muddy.
Improvements on some roads plus the increase in horsepower
began to make it possible to use the auto longer into the
winter season. A few hardy souls who had more powerful
autos with bigger wheels would break a track and others would
follow in them. Bill Mol, one of mother's cousins, operated a
garage in Silver Creek, Minnesota, which was near our home.
He was one of those hardy souls. He would put heavy duty
chains on the hind drive wheels of his large Reo auto and
break right through the snow. This wasn't always appreciated
by those who drove with the horses and bobsled. The wheels
on the car were farther apart than the runners on the bobsled.
This caused the sled to veer from right to left as first the right

runner would follow the right auto track and suddenly, when the road sloped to the left, the sled would slide over with a jerk and continue with the left runner in the left auto track. A lot of farmers thought autos should be outlawed on the road during the time of snow.

A few enterprising manufacturers tried to market a sled with runners the same distance apart as the auto's wheels. The idea was good, but not every farmer could afford a new sled just to accommodate the crazy guys who wanted to use their autos in the snow. Feelings sometimes ran high between the old timers and those young "squirts" who didn't have enough sense to keep their autos in the shed where they belonged.

In the early and mid-30s many ideas were tried to clear a track for the auto. One that worked rather well was to fasten an old walking plow to the side of one of the sled runners. We would then hook up the horses to the sled and urge them into a fast trot or even a gallop. The curved moldboard of the plow would then throw the snow five to ten feet out. By coming back on the same road, we would plow out the other track. Since the plow was fastened on the outside of the runner, it plowed a path 12 to 14 inches wider on each side of the sled track. This made it wide enough for the autos to follow. It didn't work when the drifts were real bad, only in snow up to a foot deep.

Meeting a car when there was only one double track open created quite a problem. Many times it was necessary to back up for a half mile to the nearest driveway, or to shovel an opening on each side of the track to permit the oncoming car to get by. Fortunately the traffic wasn't heavy. Also, there were places where sleds had already made tracks as they met.

4

When Boys Wore Dresses

A record of the past would not be complete without re-calling how we dressed. Clothing was made or purchased mostly on its practical value, not so much for its style. It had to combat the cold and other weather conditions, although style and custom did influence "dress up" clothes.

Babies—whether girls or boys—wore dresses until one or two years of age. These dresses were usually quite long. Boys then went into knee pants—short trousers that had a band sewed to the bottom of each leg. This band had a button and button hole on the ends that fastened just above the knee. Long black stockings and button shoes usually covered the legs and feet. Coats and shirts were not very different from those of today.

As soon as we boys approached manhood we graduated into long pants. Wearing our first suit with long pants was an intently anticipated event. It carried a symbolic meaning. We were no longer boys; we were men! I recall needing a new suit when I was 14. Mom and Pa picked out one of the largest short-pants suits that could be purchased for a boy. I was so disappointed! I had felt that I was man enough to own long pants. Buying that large knee-pants suit meant I would be wearing it for at least another two years, and I didn't think I should have to stay a boy that long.

The tradition of short pants for boys continued for many years. It wasn't until our son Lawrence was a boy that a few parents broke the tradition and long pants became acceptable for young boys. Many of the older generation frowned on the practice. They felt that long pants gave the youngsters a feeling of "cockiness" and hastened the maturation process.

As I have said, winter attire for school was purchased strictly for its practical and economical use. We wore a type of legging around each leg outside of our overalls. They were made of canvas or heavy denim. They were lined with flannel, opened on the side and were laced through a series of hooks and eyes. They were usually long enough to cover the legs from below the ankles to just below the knees. Attached to the bottom of the legging was a leather strap that passed under the foot at the instep and fastened with a buckle. These leggings could be used over leather shoes or rubber overshoes. Heavy fleece-lined underwear plus one or two overalls, a heavy coat or mackinaw, a heavy wool cap with earflaps, and, on real cold days, a long scarf around the neck and face completed the outfit. It became a five or ten minute task to dress a youngster—if he cooperated. Many teachers spent up to a full hour dressing the younger children for their long walk home.

We counted the days till spring would come and we could run outside barefooted with only an overall to cover our skin. As summer approached, heavy callouses developed underneath our feet and we walked over stones and rough roads with no pain. This practice was not without danger. Glass, thorns and other sharp objects often penetrated even the toughest callouses. Then we soaked the foot in Lysol solution and were forced to wear a shoe or rubber overshoe until the sore was healed. It was a miracle that more children did not contract tetanus, as vaccination was unknown at the time. Occasionally a child did get "lockjaw" as it was called at the time. The child seldom lived.

5

Learning in a Two-Room School

The radical change in education in the last 60 years is difficult to describe. I started classes in a two-room school. That meant four grades in each room and two teachers. There was a hall between the two rooms where we hung our coats and placed our overshoes. This hall also contained the 10-gallon drinking fountain that served all the students.

Each room contained a large pot-bellied wood stove that was surrounded by a circular metal shield about 12 inches out from the stove and the same height above the floor. The shield's purpose was to protect us from the stove, which at times was red hot, and to provide a method of circulating the air around the room. The latter didn't work too well and there were many mornings that we sat or stood around the stove for the first hour to stay warm. Monday mornings were always the worst. The fire was not kept burning during the weekend and the cold penetrated everything in the room.

School started at 9 a.m. and was excused at 4 p.m. We had a 15-minute recess morning and afternoon. The one-hour noon break was sometimes cut to a half-hour during the shorter winter days.

The fires were kindled by the teacher each morning. She was expected to get it started early enough to have the room warm by 9 a.m., but that wasn't always possible. In later years an eighth-grade boy was given the responsibility of starting the fires. This was a sought-after job since it paid 15 cents per day. I was given this dubious honor for one winter. It meant starting out an hour earlier and sitting in a cold room till the stove became hot. I recall one Monday morning the thermometer read -18° F inside the schoolroom when I got there.

The shield around the stove had a 12-inch pipe that extended through the outside wall and was intended to draw fresh air into the room. It really didn't seem necessary since the large windows permitted lots of outside air to come through the cracks. It was a favorite pastime to annoy the teacher by shouting into this vent from the outside. To be caught meant detention, but that didn't stop us from trying.

There were no lights except an old kerosene lamp that was used when the school board met, or the teacher wanted to work late. The water supply was carried by bucket from a farm about two blocks away. The pump was a shallow well situated in a corner of the farmer's hog house—not exactly the most sanitary source of drinking water. In winter we could not fill the drinking fountain until the room was warm. Each evening the overhead fountain had to be emptied to prevent the tank and pipes from freezing and breaking. In real cold weather we sometimes had just a bucket and dipper. There were times we had ice water—not by choice, but because ice had formed on the edge of the bucket.

Toilet facilities were two six-foot by six-foot "three holers," one for the girls on the north side of the school and one for the boys on the south side. They were about a hundred feet from the school building. If we had snow, a path had to be shoveled to each one—a task assigned to a group of reluctant boys. During school hours, we were permitted toilet privileges. We indicated our request by raising a hand and holding up two fingers. The teacher gave her consent if we didn't abuse the privilege.

While school was in session, everyone was quiet and we remained in our seats. We could obtain permission to whisper to someone by raising a hand and putting up only one finger. Here, too, permission was granted as long as it wasn't abused. With four classes in each room, each class was called in turn to the front to sit in two long "recitation" seats. The teacher would then ask questions, give help, or ask students to read, depending on the subject matter that was scheduled for that time. Recitation periods were usually only 15 minutes long but were changed at the discretion of the teacher

For those who remained in their seats, it took a special ability to concentrate. We sometimes found it more interesting to listen to the particular class that was reciting at the time. That could also be a learning experience. I learned a lot from the class that was above me and was able to use that knowledge the following year.

The school year was eight months long, but many boys did not attend in the fall or spring. They were needed to help with the farm work. Absenteeism was an accepted thing and no excuses were needed to return to school. You were expected to make up your work on your own time; if you didn't, it was reflected in your grades. Many of the boys quit when they discovered that the class had progressed so far that it seemed impossible to catch up. My parents valued education very highly and made a special effort to keep us in school.

A state test was given at the end of every school year to any student who wished to take it. Graduation from the eighth grade was automatic with a passing grade on these state exams regardless of which grade the student was in. When I was in the sixth grade I had a teacher named Esther Larson. She noticed that I watched the seventh and eighth grades recite and that I was able to compete successfully with them. She gave me some books to study and suggested that I take the exams.

It was necessary to travel to another school to take them because they were only given in certain schools. My parents made the special effort to get me to the school. I took the exams in all the subjects and passed them. I was then officially through school at 12 years of age in 1922.

High school was out of the question for me. It meant leaving home and boarding in town which we could not afford. Besides, I was needed at home. My parents thought it would be wise to go back during the next winter when they didn't need me so badly on the farm. I did, and took some extra eighth grade subjects. I took and passed the exams again in May. The next fall my father died, ending my school career for nearly seven years.

Several other memories come to mind. Our school library consisted of four eight-foot shelves in the corner of the room. By the time I had completed the eighth grade, I had read nearly all of them.

Discipline was strict and absolute. Teachers were permitted to use physical punishment and often did. We never reported this to our parents. That would only mean more of the same. Our report cards were marked in percentages with our deportment, or behavior, indicated by letter or a note on the bottom of the card. Many parents were more concerned about that than any of the other reports.

The teachers usually boarded in one of the homes near the school and were treated as one of the family. There were very few married teachers in the elementary country school. They usually taught a few years, then married and quit teaching. Occasionally a single woman would make it her career. I had six different teachers in the seven years I went to country school. They were paid from 25 to 35 dollars per month.

Our school had some double desks in which two students sat together. That both saved space and taught us how to get along with our neighbor. Sometimes it wasn't possible, so the teacher had to try different pairings until a compatible arrangement was found.

Recreation during recess and noon hour was nearly always outside. Only in the severest weather were we allowed to remain inside. I'm sure this was done to allow the teacher to recuperate, as she seldom had time to play with us outdoors. There was no preparation time for her except before and after school.

We played a type of scrub baseball. No sides were chosen. We all played each position and advanced from third baseman, one step at a time, as each out was made. Our school was on the shore of a 10-acre pond, so we skated if the ice was safe and clear. When the snow was too deep for skating, we played a game called "Fox and Geese." This game required a circular path in the snow, with paths to the center area called "home." Someone was selected as the fox and the rest of us were geese. The geese were to venture out from home, and if the fox tagged one, that goose became a fox. This continued until there was only one goose left, who was declared the winner.

The school being on the shore of this pond provided us with lots of recreation but was also a serious hazard. It was a concern for parents and teachers alike, especially in the spring when the run-off from the snow doubled its size.

One nearly tragic incident occurred when two boys decided to use a cake of ice about 15 feet square as a raft to ferry themselves from the shore to the main ice mass about 30 feet out in the center of the pond. They used long poles to push themselves from shore. They had reached the center piece and were on their return trip when they decided to stand close to each other on the edge of their ice raft. The other end came up and the boys, fully clothed and in heavy coats and boots, slid off into the cold water. The water was over their heads. They struggled to swim toward shore. Fortunately, there were poles lying around that we were able to cast out to them and pull them in. It was a close call to a double tragedy. One of the boys went home after getting the water out of his boots while the other one stayed by the stove. He was nearly dry by school closing time. I think we all learned a lesson. There were other times when we ventured out on thin ice and got our feet wet, but never came so close to tragedy as that one noon hour.

One of our guaranteed teacher-annoying tricks was to climb onto the roof of the school and hide between the bell tower and the peak of the roof. The culprit would take a stone with him and hit the bell until the teacher came out. The culprit's accomplice would warn him of the approaching teacher so he could quickly slip into hiding. The rest of us would be innocently playing games. It wasn't easy to determine who the guilty party was. One teacher solved the puzzle by calling the recess to a halt by ringing the bell and noting who was absent. The culprit could never get down by himself. He needed two other boys to hold his feet as he climbed up or down. The guilty party served a sentence of writing "I won't climb the bell tower" a thousand times. That put a stop to it until the next year and another teacher.

Deliberate and destructive vandalism were minimal problems. Carving someone else's initials or name on a desk did happen, but I don't recall that a window was ever deliberately broken. On Halloween, the outside toilets were usually tipped over onto their sides, until the school board put a concrete footing under them and bolted them down.

The only physical education program we had was lots of work on the farm. Even the boys in town had many chores to do. This provided an outlet for much of our excess energies. Those boys who were not interested in learning and were inclined toward mischief usually quit school before they finished the eighth grade.

Training in music was limited to singing a few songs each morning, usually something patriotic or easy songs by Stephen Foster. I don't recall any prayer or Bible reading being part of our school day, but we pledged our "allegiance to the flag" every day.

One of the highlights of each school year was the Thanksgiving or Christmas program. Sometimes we had both.

Recitations, dialogues, plays and songs were all part of the program. After our rehearsing intensively for weeks, the parents and the rest of the community were invited to see and hear what we had learned. A lunch was served afterwards. Frequently it was a basket social. Then each seventh and eighth grade girl decorated a shoe box or basket and filled it with goodies enough for two people. An auctioneer was selected and the baskets were sold to the highest bidder, usually the 16-to-20-year-old boys. The girl was supposed to share the contents with the boy who bought hers. Sometimes she would let a favorite boy in on how her basket was decorated. If the other boys caught on, the favored one had to pay a very high price to get that basket, as the others continued to bid against him. At times, a girl was too timid to sit with the successful bidder; then he ate it alone or shared it with another boy. The proceeds from the social would often go to buy some necessary articles for the school.

School methods did not start to change much until roads began to be passable in the winter. Transportation by bus to larger consolidated schools became possible then, bringing high school within the reach of many more students. Bus transportation became available about 1935. Parents were required to pay the transportation cost of four dollars per month until around 1940.

I started high school in 1930 when I was 20 years old. There was no bus transportation from our area, so I drove. I picked up Henrietta Mol, Jim Schut, Glorene Thurk and, for a time, Irene Klemz. Wilmina Schut rode with us the second year. So did my sister Elsie for a while. We found a lot of enjoyment in riding together even though the old 1927 Chevrolet did give us trouble now and then. I was older than any of the others in my class and studies were easy for me. At the end of the first year I had completed enough subjects to be classified as a junior. The third year, when I was a senior, was difficult financially. The car had caused us a lot of trouble and we couldn't afford another one. I decided to stay with a farmer near Annandale. I helped him with chores and rode the horse bus to school. I could have walked those two miles just as fast, and often did, but the enclosed bus provided protection from the weather as well as giving me an opportunity to study or visit with the other students.

When I was a junior, I was president of the class. Through the help of parents, we juniors managed to give the seniors a banquet. But when we became seniors the depression had so completely exhausted everybody's funds that the school administration decided it was impossible for the juniors to give us a banquet. Many, including myself, could not afford to buy a class ring or new clothes for graduation, so we were forced to borrow old suits or dresses from friends and relatives. A number of farm families quit sending their children to high school. Most of my peer group never went to high school. Elsie quit after or during her sophomore year. She found the adjustment from country school too difficult. Learning was not easy for her and she was not motivated enough to work as hard as she had to.

As I had been blessed with a good memory and a good mind, I was able to graduate at the top of the class. In a way, it proved to me that I had done the right thing in starting high school at 20 even though I had been the brunt of a great deal of criticism and ridicule when I first started.

My brother Bert deserved much credit for my being able to go through high school as he took over the respon-sibilities of the farm and the rest of the family. It wasn't until years later that he confided in me how he would like to have had a high school education also. Thank you very much, Bert!

6

Raising Chickens Grandma's Way

I chose this title because I feel that I am first of all addressing these memoirs to my sons and daughters. Of course, it is my hope that their children, as well as those that follow, will be interested enough to read it and consider that it was also written for them.

Yes, your Grandma—my Mom—really did know her chickens. Plymouth Rocks were her favorite breed. They were medium large with light gray and nearly black spots or stripes on each feather. From a distance they looked like odd-shaped pieces of granite walking across the farmyard. There were also Rhode Island Reds, a deep brown in color with some red feathers on their wings. And there were the White Leghorns and the Brown Leghorns, which were smaller.

According to Mom, no chicken was much good unless it had some Plymouth Rock blood in it. Both the Plymouth Rock hen and her "husband" made good soups. The hen had one drawback, though. She didn't lay many eggs per year. She would lay 15 to 20 and then promptly quit and become broody. A broody hen is the epitome of crabbiness. Her sole aim is to set on some eggs until they hatch. The Leghorns did not become broody as often, nor were they good mothers.

It was no easy task to raise chicks to adult chickens. Occasionally a hen would hide her eggs, hatch them out and raise a dozen chicks without any aid, but this haphazard method did not produce enough to replace those that died or found their way into the soup kettle.

Mom had a small shed with a row of eight nests on each side. She would carefully select, by size and shape, 12 to 15 eggs for each hen. As soon as she had enough broody hens, she would place these eggs in the nests and set the hens on them. Little care was necessary for the next three weeks. Mom just kept feed and water available on the floor and the hens took care of themselves. Sometimes a hen would get tired of her job and let the eggs get cold. If this were discovered soon enough, another broody hen was "happy" to be pressed into service, or else the eggs were distributed under the other hens. If those eggs had become too cold, they were destroyed, as the chicks in them would die. If a hen left her nest more than a half-hour on a cold day the eggs would no longer be worth keeping.

When the production of eggs was desired, the tendency of these hens to become broody was a distinct dis-advantage. I used to gather eggs, and when the hens became broody they would peck at my hands as I tried to retrieve the eggs from under them. Frequently, I would take a stick and try to chase or coax them off their nests, but those hens were quite persistent and really cranky.

Any broody hens that were not needed to set on eggs were confined in an open-air crate with no nests in it, only feed and water. They would be over their broody spell within two or three days and would start laying again in another week or so. After laying 15 or 20 eggs, they would decide it was time to set again and once more become broody. This cycle continued during most of the summer.

Hatching out the eggs and raising their young was a full summer's job for the hens that had been selected to do so. After the chicks were one or two days old, the mother hen and chicks were moved into small individual coops about two feet square. We had a couple of six-unit coops with a hen and chicks in each unit. The roof was made of boards with a strip of roofing over it to shed the rain. The sides and back were solid lumber, but the front had one-and-a-half-inch slats nailed vertically from top to bottom. These slats were far enough apart to allow the chicks to get out but kept the mother hen inside. This was done to prevent the hen from making a home for her chicks in an unsuitable place. After two or three weeks, the hen was allowed out to range around the farm and find food for her flock. During the first days it took some persuasion to get the family to return "home," but after that they were usually home by dark.

It was an interesting pastime to watch a mother hen and her chicks. She knew which chicks belonged to her and woe to any neighbor's chicks coming near them. The mother hen was out with her family at the first ray of dawn. She would immediately start scratching in the straw, ground, or grass, and when she found a worm, a kernel of corn, or an insect, she would pounce on it. Then she would call her chicks by issuing a sharp "click, click" or "clack, clack." The chicks would come running and first come, first served. They soon learned their mother's methods and could find some of their own food.

Not every chick lived to maturity, as there were many dangers present. One was our big gray cat who liked chicks for dinner—or, for that matter, for breakfast or lunch. He was no match for the mother hen, though. If she saw him anywhere near, she ruffled up her feathers to twice her size, then charged at him with beak and claws until he decided it would be less dangerous to stalk a mouse or gopher.

If the small coops were left unprotected at night, rats and skunks would create havoc. A long board placed in front of the slats each evening discouraged them from entering.

Hawks and crows were ever-present dangers during the day, but the mother hen had her eye cocked at all times. At the slightest sign of danger, she would screech out a warning and all the chicks would dive for cover or crawl under their mother's wings until her "all clear" signal was given. As the chicks grew larger, the mother hen would no longer be able to cover the entire brood. It was a comical sight to see all those small heads protruding from every side of her. When the chicks became larger yet, it was sometimes difficult for her to keep her feet on the ground and she would more or less "float" on a couple dozen legs.

Another two or three months and the chicks were nearly independent of the hen. They were able to forage for themselves. Foraging was supplemented by grain twice a day, a mixture of cracked corn, oats and wheat. In later years, those grains were ground and mixed with a high protein feed such as bran or meat scraps. This was made into a mash and placed into self-feeders where the chicks just helped themselves. It cost more money, but the chickens matured faster. Also, it considerably lessened the dangers of their picking up a disease from the ground.

As it is nearly impossible to distinguish between male and female chicks when they are first hatched, Mom permitted them all to grow up together. The ratio of the two sexes was approximately one to one. With chickens being polygamists by nature (one rooster would take care of 12 to 15 hens), there were always more roosters than we needed for mating purposes. The surplus roosters landed in the soup kettle or frying pan. Our Sunday dinners were usually chicken. We all thought our mother made the best chicken soup in Wright County. I haven't changed my mind about that even though my wife can make a super delicious soup that is quite comparable.

In Grandma's day the chicken and egg production project was primarily a woman's domain. Pa would clean out the henhouse when it was necessary, and carry in clean straw, but the rest of the work was Mom's responsibility.

Chickens were always lousy in those days. After gathering

eggs or handling the chicks, we usually had to wash the lice off our hands and arms before they had a chance to travel too far up our sleeves. We sprayed the nests and roosts periodically with a creosote solution to discourage the lice from harboring there. Also, once or twice a year, we would catch each hen and dust her with lice powder. That would decrease the lice population considerably, but never down to zero. At any rate, our efforts made the hens healthier and more comfortable, and we were rewarded with more eggs.

Surplus eggs were sold. Farm wives usually had the freedom to spend this "egg money" as they wished. It usually went for a new dress or other clothing.

There was a popular joke that went the rounds about that time. It seems that the treasurer of the Ladies' Aid brought a substantial amount of Aid money into the bank. She told the banker, "This is Aid money." The banker understood her to say "This is egg money," and he remarked, "Well, it looks like the old hens are doing quite well this year."

As the story goes, it took some explaining to smooth all the ruffled feathers.

7

Vet en Stroop
& Other Memorable Foods

What did we eat when I was young? Many things that would
cause modern-day youngsters—and probably many modern-
day oldsters, too—to turn up their noses. True, our tastes have
changed considerably, but the methods of preparing food
have changed even more.

Because America has always been the melting pot of many
nationalities and races, both the foods and the eating habits of
the people of our country are a mixture of the contributions
from many lands.

Our parents came from a Holland-Dutch ancestry, so they
shared many foods that were particularly Dutch. Not only that,
but they also came from Gelderland, a specific province in
Holland. The people of each province had their own special
recipes, too. Add to that the fact that some families prepared
their foods in a way that no other family did and you could
find quite a variety. Fortunately, with ancestors of both my
parents coming from Gelderland, Mom did not have to
"train" Pa to eat any new kinds of dishes. He was already
acquainted with them and liked them. That wasn't always the
case when the wife came from one province and the husband
from another. The problem became even more complicated
for couples whose ancestry originated in different countries.

With the mobility of today, we can order many foods from
other countries or go to restaurants which specialize in foods
of a given nationality.

The food that Mom set on our table was simple, but it was ample and nutritious. I'm sure most of today's children would complain, "Is *that* all we get to eat?" Perhaps some of the vitamins or minerals we now consider essential were lacking, but our stomachs were filled and we grew.

Basically, we had cooked oatmeal for breakfast, with an egg if the chickens were laying. That was usually during the summer. The coop was so cold in the winter that the hens "went on vacation." Also, the breeds we had in those days were able to produce only a fraction of the number of eggs that the chickens do today.

We ate side pork for breakfast during the winter. Mom also made a Dutch dish which was simply fresh pork fat poured on our plate to which we added syrup. We would then take a slice of Mom's homemade bread, break off a small piece, dip it into the mixture and eat it. This was called *vet en stroop* (fat and syrup).

Sometimes we made a game of the process. By not mixing the fat into the syrup, but dipping the bread into each, one at a time, the ratio between the two ingredients could be manipulated so they would not come out even. Mom and Pa tried to limit our consumption somewhat, but we always came out with either too much syrup or too much fat and had to add more of whichever was used up. Then we would have too much of that! Our trick never worked more than once or twice at a sitting because Pa or Mom would say, "That's all you get. You better make it come out even." And so we did.

Other times, Mom would make a milk gravy from the meat fat. Again, we would break up a slice of bread and pour the gravy over it on our plate. This was a very tasty and filling dish.

We always had all the raw milk we wanted, though it was seldom real cold. The only refrigeration we had was "winter." Coffee was a luxury for adults only. Fruit juice for breakfast was unknown to us until I was over 30 years old. I do recall tasting grapefruit for the first time when I was 18 and confined to the hospital. I remember thinking it was too bitter to eat.

I had no idea that dry, "ready-to-eat" cereal even existed until one time we visited Aunt Nell Tubergen. She filled our bowls with "Grape Nuts," but none of us would eat it. I think I was about 10 years old at the time. "Corn Flakes" and "Wheaties" became acceptable breakfast food for us when I was 15 or 20 years old, but only as a treat. Oatmeal and wheat grits remained the old standby.

In some homes, the husband would have a cup of coffee immediately after he got up in the morning. This was usually prepared by the wife, who had to get up a little earlier to build a fire in the wood stove and boil water for the coffee. After a cup or two, the husband would go out to the barn to milk the cows. The wife would come shortly after to help.

In our home, Pa got up first and went directly to the barn. Mom helped milk only during the spring rush season and during harvest. Pa would come for his breakfast after he had completed the milking and had brought the milk to the house for separating. The cream separator stood in the house in the winter and on the porch during the summer. It did a better job of separating the cream from the milk when the milk was still warm, so that operation was done very soon after milking. If there was enough help, we would start the machine while the last cow was being milked. After that chore was done we could have breakfast. In the summer, we were often finished with breakfast by 6:30 or 7:00 a.m. Pa would take the skim milk to the hogs or calves and complete the chores. He would then curry the horses, put on their harnesses and go to the field to work.

Coffee break came about 10 o'clock in the morning when the wife or children would bring the coffee and a couple of slices of bread with either jelly or meat on them to the field.

The horses welcomed this break as much as the farmer. I

once had a couple of horses who would double their speed when they saw someone with the lunch bucket at the end of the field. They also seemed to have a built-in time clock. About 11:30 a.m., they would speed up on the end of the field near home, hoping I would go in for dinner. It sometimes took quite a bit of persuading to convince them there was time for another round or two. Their pace became considerably slower until we came around on the homeward stretch again.

Before we could go in for dinner, the horses had to be given a drink, their bridles removed, and be taken into their stalls and fed. They got a gallon of grain plus a forkful of hay. If it was hot out we had to be careful that the horses didn't drink too much water. That would make them sick. We had one horse who used to stick his head into the water way up to his eyes to cool off.

Noon meals were called dinners. They were usually quite large, consisting of potatoes, meat, gravy, a vegetable and coffee or milk. Dessert would be a fruit sauce, pie or pudding. Salads, as we know them today, were unknown to us. Mealtimes were very busy during grain threshing time.

At first, when I was a boy, the grain was stacked and a crew of seven to ten went from farm to farm with a steam engine and threshing machine. They threshed the grain at a certain price per bushel. They usually carried their own blankets and slept in the haymow on a pile of hay or straw. They ate all their meals in the family kitchen where a long table was pulled out from wall to wall. At times there were 15 men around the table. The women served them first. After they had eaten, the women and we children would eat. There were usually several women helping with the food preparation. Sometimes teenaged girls were hired. At other times, the wives of the neighbors helped each other. As I said, it was a busy time and usually a hot one. The cooking was done on the kitchen stove using wood for fuel. Some farm homes had a summer kitchen. In that case, the cooking was done out there instead of in the kitchen-dining room. The excitement and good food, along with the good-humored fellowship around the table, made threshing time an event we talked about for weeks. It is a memory I will never forget.

In later years, more threshing machines came into the country and it became possible to shock-thresh the grain. This meant that, instead of hauling the shocks out of the field and stacking them into stacks to await the threshing machine, we would haul the bundles out of the shocks on wagons (also called racks) to wherever the farmer wanted his straw piled and would throw them from the wagon into the thresher. Six or eight neighbors, with their sons and hired men, would band together and help each other. When one job was done, the threshing rig and "crew" would move on to the next helper's farm. It took a larger crew than we had with stack-threshing, because the machine had to be kept operating at full capacity at all times, and it was often a long haul from shock to stack. Frequently, there were 20 men and boys that would eat in shifts. Shock-threshing did eliminate quite a number from the breakfast table, though, as the neighbors who helped ate their breakfast at home.

Harvest days were long and often hot. The family was up long before daylight to do the chores and prepare the huge meals for the day. A couple of pails of potatoes were peeled, 15 to 20 loaves of bread had to be mixed and baked, and stacks of dishes were everywhere! It was often 11 p.m. before everything was cleaned up after supper.

Not having the conveniences of today's modern kitchens made threshing time a nightmare to many a housewife. Also, the constant flow of people through the screen doors, the heat from the stove, and the smell of the food made the kitchen a literal fly haven. There was no way to keep them out. Fly spray was unknown, and the sheets of sticky flypaper were quickly blackened with flies and had to be replaced daily. Swatters were in constant use. But for all the papers and swatters, it wasn't unusual to find flies in the gravy, eggs or vegetables, but they had been sterilized and were dead, so they caused little fuss. Nor did anyone notice the smell of horses, cows, hogs, grain-smut and sweat that permeated the air. We were all so accustomed to the odors that our noses had been desensitized to them.

When silo-filling became popular, the same feeding process was repeated, except on a smaller scale. Ditto for corn-shredding time, only this was in the fall and the cooler weather made it easier to cope with the flies and the heat. But more details about these farm operations in a later chapter. . .

Winter brought considerable changes in both food preparations and our eating habits. When the temperatures settled below freezing, a hog or steer was butchered and cut up into pieces and the meat was frozen on an outside porch. It was then stored in animal-proof boxes or barrels. Too often, though, man's best plans were thwarted by cats and dogs. Many a pound of good meat found its way into the stomachs of "Tommy" and "Rover."

Meat for the summer's use was canned, salted, fried in lard, or home-cured and smoked. The canning was done in quart jars, cooked for three hours, then sealed. It was a good way to preserve the meat and the flavor was excellent. Salting pork did preserve the meat well, but the salt had to be soaked out before cooking and much of the flavor went out with it. I'm sure not many people would come for a second time if they were offered this meat for dinner.

Curing and smoking the ham, bacon and dried beef was a long process, but it led to a good tasty product. When this method was used, the meat had to be soaked in salt brine for two to six weeks, depending upon the size of the piece. The brine was made by adding salt to the water until a fresh egg would float in the solution.

We had a small smokehouse, about eight feet square, in which there was an old stove but no stovepipe or chimney.

After salt-curing the meat, we would make a good fire in the stove and create a bed of hot coals. On this, we would dump a shovelful of dry sawdust. If possible, we used hickory or maple sawdust. It took three to six days more to create the correct cure and taste. The smokehouse had cracks in the sides, and the smoke coming out through them made it look as though the smokehouse were on fire. Of course the stove prevented the fire from burning the shed down. Sometimes we smoked meat for several neighbors. Then the rows of bacon and hams made almost any mouth drool.

I should mention one man who had a slaughterhouse on his farm. He butchered animals a couple days per week all summer long. He also had an insulated wagon drawn by a team of horses. With ice cakes inside to keep the meat cool, he would drive from farm to farm selling fresh meat. Because he was clean and conscientious, he had a thriving business. His meat was quite costly compared to that raised and prepared on each individual farm. This could come from animals that had cost nothing except the hay and grain grown by the farmer.

Butchering a hog was not a simple task with the primitive tools we had then. I know. I butchered many of them for ourselves and for neighbors. I don't know where I learned how, except by watching others and by trial and error (mostly error at first).

It took two men nearly half a day to prepare for and actually butcher a hog. We had to fill a 15-gallon boiler that Mom used for heating her wash water and bring it to boiling. The water on our farm was very "hard" from the minerals in the soil, so we added lye (sodium hydroxide) to precipitate them out and make the water "soft." Sometimes wood ashes, which contain chemicals that soften water, were used.

While the water was heating, we would prepare a platform of boards outside under a tree or in the doorway of a shed. Then we blocked a 50-gallon wooden barrel firmly against the platform at about a 45-degree angle. We would also hang a rope and a series of pulleys overhead from a tree limb or a beam of the shed. From the bottom pulley we hung either a wooden or steel bar about 24 inches long that had hooks on each end. We were now ready to rope and bring the unwilling victim next to the platform.

The details of what would follow will not please a squeamish person. If you happen to be one who would rather not indulge, may I suggest you skip the next several paragraphs and rejoin me at the start of the next chapter?

To continue, for those who are interested in knowing just how the job was done, we would take the hog, which was no easy task, throw it on its back, and hold it down with our knees. I would then have to "stick" the hog, which meant driving a sharp knife into its throat to cut off his jugular vein. We had to hold the hog like this until it had bled to death. It may seem like a cruel method, but to kill the animal by any other means we had available at the time would have permitted the blood to remain in the meat tissues. This would have made it much more difficult to preserve.

After the hog was dead, we would place it on the platform, go after the boiler of hot water and empty it into the slop barrel. Because overly hot water would have cooked the skin, we usually threw in about a half gallon of cold water, too. We would then place the dead hog, head first, into the barrel and slowly pull it in and out of the hot water, turning the animal as we went. All we wanted to do was scald the skin until the hair would pull out easily, then we turned the hog around, put a heavy steel hook in his jaw, and placed his rear end in the barrel until that hair was also loose. This all had to happen very quickly or the water would become too cold to use.

After the scalding was completed, we would lay the steaming hog on the platform again and use scrapers to remove the hair. These scrapers were fashioned much like a garden hoe with only an eight-inch handle. If the scalding had been done properly, it would take us only 20 or 30 minutes to remove all the hair. Sometimes there were parts of the skin that had not been scalded enough. Then we would have to use a sharp knife and shave the hair off those places. That left some of our bacon with short whiskers on the rind.

After all the hair had been removed, the rope and pulleys were lowered and the hooks on the crosspieces were hooked around the tendons of the hog's hind legs. We could then hoist the hog off the platform with his head hanging about six inches from the ground. In this position, it was a simple matter to cut off the head and eviscerate the carcass.

Many of the internal organs were kept for food, including the heart, liver, and sometimes the kidneys. Mom would often remove all the fat from the intestines so it could be used in making soap. Also, if sausages were to made, the intestines were cleaned with a weak lye solution and later used as a casing for the sausages.

After the hog had been cleaned out and thoroughly washed, we would hoist it up with the rope and pulleys to hang for several hours out of reach of the dogs and cats. When it was cool, we cut the carcass into halves and then quarters with a sharp, heavy cleaver.

The cutting and processing, by freezing, salting or canning, took at least another day or two, depending on the size of the hog.

8

A Time to Live
& a Time to Die

Even though we lived on a farm, Pa did not let me witness the birth of a pig or calf until I was nearly 12 years old. The first time came about more from necessity than by design. It happened when a gilt (mother hog) was having difficulty delivering one of her pigs. Pa had tried to reach into the birth canal, but his hand was too large. Because my hand was smaller, he drafted me to reach in and pull the little one out by its head. I was amazed, to say the least. After that, Pa told me much about the processes of conception, pregnancy and the birth of animals, but he never translated those facts into terms of human reproduction.

These mysteries were perhaps the best kept secrets of the time. It is almost unbelievable that my brother Bill's arrival shortly after the pig incident was a complete surprise to me. I do remember having commented to Mom, "You're getting fat," but she had just shrugged it off. As she was naturally quite fat at that time, and wore loose clothing, her pregnancy probably wasn't very noticeable.

A person's arrival into the world has never been a simple process. The cost of lives both maternal and in stillbirths is high even today. By the standards of earlier years, however, the price has dropped tremendously.

Uncle Rick Hullman brought Aunt Hen to help with the first

birth in our family. When she was finally out of the bedroom, Uncle Rick shouted, "I knew it! Is it a boy or a girl?"

"Keep still!" Aunt Hen whispered. "The child is dead."

"Oh, I didn't know," Uncle Rick replied, "and I'm sorry."

Mom had been through a very difficult time. She was lying at death's door from the loss of blood. A young doctor from Maple Lake had been called to help deliver the baby but had found the case too much for him to handle alone. His colleague from Annandale was called, but the trip by buggy had taken too long. My oldest brother was born dead.

The birth of a child always took place in the home, many times without a doctor. Very little care was given to the mother either before or after. Doctors were severely handicapped at the time of delivery. Their anesthetics were rather primitive, and they had only minimum utensils for sterilizing the few available instruments.

The baby was always well cared for. It never lacked the most important ingredient for raising a child—love. The grandparents, uncles, aunts, cousins, brothers, sisters, and neighbors all vied for the honor of holding the child.

Mother's milk was the only food it had for the first months of life. There were no baby foods or formulas as such. The gradual transition from mother's milk to adult foods took place more according to family tradition than by order of a doctor.

An integral part of every baby's clothing was the navel band. This was a band of white cloth, usually flannel, about three inches wide, that was wrapped around the baby's abdomen. It was held tightly in place by safety pins. The purpose of the band was to prevent a navel hernia. It was worn for months after the stem of the umbilical cord was healed. Boys were not circumcised unless it was necessary to permit free passage of urine.

There were many dangerous hurdles for a child to overcome. The danger of accidental death was perhaps not the greatest, but injuries from farm animals and falls from hay-lofts, trees and the like did take their toll in both life and limb.

Tetanus, or "lockjaw" as it was called at that time, was an ever-present hazard when an injury occurred. There were several good products on the market to help prevent infection. Lysol solution, Epsom salts (magnesium sulfate), or hydrogen peroxide were some of the effective antiseptics we used for soaking a wound.

By far the most dangerous hurdles were the many contagious childhood diseases. They sometimes wiped out entire families of children. Whooping cough seldom killed, but complications of pneumonia often did. Measles, mumps, and chicken pox, as well as scarlet fever, polio, and diphtheria, were also threats until a youngster was through his or her teens. Pinkeye also gave much trouble.

The most dreaded were, perhaps, diphtheria and polio. There was no protection against them so they took many lives. We knew of only a few cases of smallpox because a vaccine was available for it. Tuberculosis was also a killer, although it was not as contagious as some of the others. Many people died of it even in adult life.

Laws concerning contagious diseases were strict.

"You must stay home," the township clerk said, as he nailed the large white sign to our door. "Someone else must milk your cows, wash your cream separator and deliver your cream to the creamery until your doctor gives you permission to resume your work and permits you to leave your home."

The dreaded word "QUARANTINE" stood out in large black letters. Underneath were the words "Scarlet Fever." "No one except the doctor or a person with the doctor's permission may enter this house," it continued, "and all occupants must not associate with others who are not exposed to scarlet fever, nor may they touch any food offered for sale to the general public."

We had been to Aunt Artie's for a visit. Jim was sick in bed, but was well enough to permit Bert J., the rest of the family and me to play games with him. The next day Jim was covered with a rash and had a high temperature. Several others in the community had been afflicted also, and the disease had spread rapidly from family to family. Most adults were immune because of their having had even a light case of it in their youth. A very few escaped the disease through natural immunity.

About a week or ten days after our visit to Aunt Artie, Bert and I were sleeping upstairs when he woke up with nausea, high fever, and a sore throat, the three sure-fire symptoms of scarlet fever. I was 19 years old and Bert was 17. As I had just recovered from a three-month siege with a broken appendix, surgery, pneumonia and phlebitis, the doctor said I wouldn't get scarlet fever now. "Your body has built up an immunity against everything for at least a year," he explained. "No germ will be able to invade your system and survive."

Mom decided to try keeping the disease limited to Bert. She had heard that if a curtain were laced over the doorway and kept partially saturated with Lysol, and if all the utensils that Bert used were kept sterilized, it might be possible to contain the germ and prevent it from spreading. She must also let no one but herself (she was immune because she'd had it when she was young) go into Bert's room.

Scarlet fever was known to be a serious disease. Fatal complications often set in. Kidney failure and pneumonia were usually the cause of death. Bed rest and a person's own defense were the only cure we had.

Mother did succeed in limiting the illness to Bert. The rest of us were only bored because we had just each other to play with. I couldn't even go to the barn.

The cows had to be milked and the chores had to be done, so we hired a man. Henry Wolf, a nephew of our neighbors, the Dykhuizens, was able to stay in their home and just walk across the road to our farm to do the chores. Fortunately, it was winter and no field work had to be done.

Even though mother was able to limit the disease, many people were afraid to talk to the rest of us who were well. Not even outside. Bert wasn't sick for long, and since he was the only one to become affected, our quarantine sign didn't stay on the door as long as Aunt Artie's. Her family contracted the disease one at a time from each other, prolonging the siege. Tired of being cooped up, Bert and I decided to ski through the fields to their home. On our way, we met some distant neighbors who were on the road.

"Has your quarantine been lifted?" they shouted.

"No," we hollered back, "but we aren't going anywhere except to Aunt Artie's. They already have it over there."

"That's against the law," they answered, and proceeded to give us a good tongue-lashing.

We paid very little attention to them. We felt if mother could keep the disease away from us, living within the same house, there couldn't be much danger of spreading it across hundreds of feet of fresh outside air.

Pneumonia, from any cause, was a fearful disease. It usually started with a bad cold, as it does now, but there was no medicine to interrupt its course. Complete bed rest, mustard plaster on the chest, and a strong constitution were needed to survive. Pneumonia had a series of crises, at which times the disease would either become worse or get better. This often happened on the third day of a mild case, but it was usually not until the ninth. The patient would then get a high fever. If the fever broke quickly, the road to recovery was often quite rapid. Sometimes, however, the fever would continue. Then delirium and death would likely follow. Only those who have lived through the agonies of seeing a loved one suffer the ravages of pneumonia can really appreciate the blessings of today's antibiotic drugs.

I don't think people were so health conscious then as they are now. I can't recall owning a toothbrush when I was young, or ever using tooth paste until I was a teenager. We paid a high price for that neglect. I lost my four incisor front teeth before I was twenty and brother Bert had a full top plate at that age or soon after.

Vitamins were practically unknown, but we got them in our food and never worried about "tired blood" or our system's being "iron poor." We had no concern for foods that contained cholesterol. We didn't even know what it was. As for tranquilizers, the only ones we knew were hard work and fresh air, and we used lots of that!

In my parents' day, contraceptives were hardly known and their use was considered immoral. In Hazel's and my married life, there was limited acceptance of the methods then known, but many doctors refused to prescribe them or encourage their use. Large families were considered a part of married life. The problem of supporting children and giving them an education was of little concern, because children were considered financial assets. After 10 or 12 years of age they could contribute to the needs of the family either by helping at home or by working for others and sharing their earnings with their parents. This practice was expected by many parents until the child reached 21 or was married.

Death was a fact of life. There were very few families where the "grim reaper" had not taken one of the family before adulthood. In some ways it was expected. The struggle to maintain life was not as important as it seems today.

Hospitals were usually owned by doctors in private medicine. They were five- to ten-bed size in some of the larger towns in the county, while larger ones were to be found only in the big cities. About the only reason for going to a hospital was for surgery. Some operations were still being done in the home.

Since the sick and the old usually stayed at home, deaths usually took place there. We had no funeral parlors. The mortician merely took the body into his preparation room. When the body was ready, he placed it in the casket and brought it back to the home. A room was emptied of all furnishings and the body would lie in state for one to three days until the funeral took place.

During the time the body was in the home, black crepe paper or cloth was fastened to the door and friends would come to pay their respects. At night, the neighbors would take turns and stay awake all night as a tribute to the departed one. I recall a couple of neighbors who stayed in our home when my father died. They played cards all night, but that was not considered disrespectful.

On the day of the funeral, a short service was held in the home for the close relatives. After that, the body was moved to the church for the final services. It was the practice to open the casket for a last time after the service, before going to the cemetery. This was done to give the family a last opportunity to see the body. All the male members of the immediate family wore black arm bands above their elbows for a few weeks or more as a symbol of mourning. The ladies wore black veils around their hats and some let them hang down in front of their faces.

9

Hazel's Ancestry
& Life Before Our Marriage

Most of what I have written so far is a record of my family and my life before I was married. Hazel Jane Dalman was only a name of a girl that went to our church until I was 17 when she became more than a name. I was 20 before I realized that she was becoming a very important person in my life. I must take some time to record the ancestry and events in the life of my wife, Hazel Jane Dalman.

The Dalman family emigrated from Holland many generations ago. In fact, before the Civil War, as one of Hazel's ancestors fought in that war. Very little is known about the first generations that moved to America except that they settled around Holland, Michigan, and were probably some of the earliest settlers of that area.

Hazel's grandpa, Geert (Gerrit in English) Dalman, was born in 1855, somewhere in Michigan, and married Gertee (Gertrude in English) Vork. The Vork family had emigrated from Holland one or two generations before 1859, the year that Hazel's grandma was born. It is not known whether they settled in Michigan or not. Both of Hazel's paternal grandparents had ancestors from several different provinces in Netherland, such as: Drenthe, Soest, Groningen and others. It is known for sure that Hazel's paternal grandparents were married in Michigan and that their first three children were born there. There were 11 children altogether. From the oldest to the youngest, their names and years of birth were: Ralph-1879, Jake-1881, Martin (Hazel's father)-1884, Albert-1886, John-1888, Frank-1890, Alice (Nieken)-1892, Fannie (Hoekstra)-1895, Henry-1897, and Ella Mae-1901. One son, George, died in infancy. Albert was killed by lightning while still a young man.

In 1885, Hazel's grandfather and grandmother moved with their three young sons (Martin was one year old) to Thule, South Dakota. Thule was between Eureka and Herreid, near the middle of the state's northern boundary. It has since disappeared. Hazel's grandfather and several others of the Vork family traveled by train up to Eureka, then by covered wagon for 25 miles, and claimed a homestead in that area. They built a sod shanty in which they lived for several years. Because drought and grasshoppers destroyed nearly all their crops, they were forced to leave their homestead and land. Their next home was in Sandstone, Minnesota. The chapter "Grandpa Dalman's Memory Lane" (taken from a cassette tape that he, Hazel's father, recorded in 1973 when he was 88 years old) describes quite vividly some of the hardships they encountered while living in Dakota.

Hazel's father (Martin Dalman) has told us that he and his brother Jake, both in their teens at the time, drove a team of horses in front of a wagon filled with tools, etc., all the way from Eureka to Sandstone. It took them over two weeks to make that trip of over three hundred miles. They were always welcomed and fed at farm homes where they stopped each night along the way.

Around 1903, after living in Sandstone for a year or two, the family moved again. This time it was to a farm about three miles north of Maple Lake, Minnesota. There things began to improve and Hazel's grandfather became a relatively successful farmer. He finally retired to a small farm a half mile closer to Maple Lake. He died in 1932. Hazel's

grandmother had died in 1928. They are both buried in Lakeview Cemetery about three miles south and west of Silver
Creek, Minnesota, or about two or three miles north and east
of their last home.

Hazel's maternal grandparents were John Klynstra and Jane
Kerkstra. The ancestries of both families go back to Vriesland,
Holland. John and Jane first met around Westfield, North
Dakota. The Kerkstras had lived near Holland, Nebraska, in
1882. Some went to Prairie View, Kansas, before their move to
North Dakota, and Hazel still has relatives living in those two
states. Her maternal grandparents, John and Jane Klynstra,
moved from North Dakota to Hinckley, Minnesota, sometime
in the early 1900s. Her grandfather died there at a relatively
young age and is buried in the cemetery east of Hinckley.

There were seven children in the Klynstra family: John Jr.;
Henry; Catherine "Katie" (Dalman), Hazel's mother; Peter
"Pete"; Annie (Heun); Henrietta (Brown), and Joseph "Jo."

Before her marriage, Hazel's mother had worked for a
family in North Dakota where some of the members were
afflicted with tuberculosis. At the time that Martin Dalman met
and married Catherine Klynstra, she seemed to be well, but she
had contracted tuberculosis. Hazel was two and a half years
old and her sister, Sylvia, was one when their mother died.
Hazel's father had tried hard to save her. He had taken her to
Bethesda Sanatorium in Denver, Colorado, but the disease had
progressed too far. So the family returned to Hinckley,
Minnesota, where Hazel's mother died and is buried. She died
July 4, 1915.

Hazel went to live with her Grandfather and Grandmother
Dalman in their home north of Maple Lake. Sylvia went to
live with their grandmother, Mrs. John Klynstra, in Hinckley,
Minnesota.

When Hazel was seven years old, her father remarried to
Agnes Gjein and they made their home in Strasburg, North
Dakota. Soon after a daughter, Mildred, was born. Hazel went

to live with them. After seven months, she and her grand-
parents became so lonesome for each other, it was decided that
Hazel should return and make her home with them until she
was mature. They gave her a good home. Hazel's father and
Agnes had five more children: Vernon, Harvey, Harold,
Kenneth, and Lester.

Hazel received her schooling in the Vandergon school, four
miles north of Maple Lake. This school was torn down after
the "country district" consolidated with the Maple Lake
school. Hazel completed the eighth grade and wanted to go to
high school, but her grandfather would not give his consent
because there were no buses and she would have to stay in
Maple Lake. He did allow her to receive piano lessons. She
had to drive to Maple Lake with a horse and buggy. "Dick"
was an old plug horse who had only one speed—slow—so
Hazel spent a great deal of time on the road.

When Hazel was 13 years old, her Grandmother Dalman
died. Hazel continued to live with her grandfather and to keep
house for him until she was 16. At that time, her grandfather
sold his small farm and went to live with his son and family,
Frank and Anna Dalman. They were living on the old farm
that the Dalman family had purchased in the early 1900s. It
was there that her Grandfather Dalman died.

Hazel was without a permanent home. Although she worked
for many different farm families, she made her home with
Jake and Ella Mae Mol, who lived on the south shore of Sugar
Lake. Ella Mae was Hazel's aunt, but since Hazel had lived
with her grandparents when Ella Mae was still at home, she
seemed more like a sister. She was only 11 years older than
Hazel. There was a deep and lasting bond between Hazel and
her uncle and aunt, and they treated her like their own
daughter.

Hazel worked for John and Jennie Smith, the Topfer
brothers, Dick and Alice Rozenberg, Rev. Van Egmond and at
many other places. She usually helped with house cleaning or

did the housework when the wife and mother was sick.

I had my first date with Hazel when she was still living with her grandfather. Grandpa said she was too young for dates with the same young man, so after three times, there were no more for several years. She dated several different boys and I dated other girls, but I had my eye on her. I had not given up on the possibility of dating her again. The fact that she was one of the few girls that had refused a date with me made her all the more desirable. The time did come when I got up enough nerve to ask her again. It came about partly by chance and partly by design.

Hazel was working for John Smith, who lived only a short distance from my Aunt Artie Schut. It so happened that my cousin, Henry W. Schut, would quite often take her back to John Smith's on his way home from our church.

One Sunday evening Henry W. was doing his good deed and, I'm quite sure, enjoying it. It happened to be Mrs. Smith's birthday. Many relatives and neighbors had come to help her celebrate. Aunt Artie was among them.

I had quite frequently taken Bert W. Schut and his sister, Alice, home when Henry W. had other plans, so the most logical place for me to take them was to John Smith's. When we got there, we all climbed in the car with Henry W., his girl friend, and Hazel. We all spent a pleasant evening together. This happened several times on different occasions, until Henry W. accused me of using him as bait so I could be with Hazel. There were no bad feelings between Henry W. and me at any time. It wasn't long before I discovered that Hazel was willing to have me take her home by myself. Henry W. always chided me by saying, "If it wasn't for me, you never would have gotten Hazel."

"I would have gotten her sooner or later anyway," I would reply. I must admit he may have been a link in the chain of events that brought Hazel and me together again after over two years of our dating others.

Dating each other posed many problems for us. Since she had no permanent home, I had to take her "home" to many different places. Also, I was still going to high school and had a lot of studying to do. Besides that, I was helping brother Bert with the farm work at times.

That was when our family owned the old 1927 Chevrolet sedan. It had to serve as transportation for Mother, sister Elsie, brothers John and Bill (who were in grade school), brother Bert and me. Bert and I had to double-date or arrange our dates on different days. At times this caused some friction, but it never caused any lasting hurt feelings.

One of the biggest problems we had was the terrible shortage of money. I don't know how we managed with six mouths to feed and trying to get an education for John, Bill, Elsie and myself. I could not afford to take Hazel to any event that cost money, so we would quite frequently visit relatives. We also went to many church activities and to parties in the homes of friends.

I seldom knew where Hazel would be from one week to the next and our dating was limited to once or twice a week at the most.

As the depression became more severe in 1933-34, there was very little work for Hazel, except for room and board. When she learned that housework, as a maid, was available in Minneapolis, she went to work in the homes of people there. The pay per week was two to five dollars plus board and room, with one afternoon off.

After Hazel started working in the city, dating became even more difficult. I had no money to buy gas for such a long trip, and the 50-mile bus trip home would have cost her two days wages. Consequently, we just didn't see each other for a month or more at a time. It wasn't what we wanted, but there was no alternative. When I left to go to college in Pella, Iowa, Hazel stayed in Minneapolis.

In January 1934, in the middle of the school year, she took

a bus to Pella and found work with a farm family, Dick and Agnes Ver Ploeg. They lived about six miles north of town, so I could not get out there very often. When I could, I would borrow Joe Eernissee's Ford coupe and put in one gallon of gas (I had no money for more). Hazel often gave me money from the two dollars per week that she earned so I could come back the next week.

She worked hard for the Ver Ploegs from February to July 1934. As I had to leave for home in June, we didn't see each other again until she came back to Maple Lake. She started working in Minneapolis again in August, and we saw each other once or twice a month. We also wrote to each other once or twice a week unless she came out or I went to see her in the city.

It was during the following summer (1935) that we decided to be married on September fourth of that year—a decision we never regretted.

Above: John Schut (father), Bert, Henry (author), Elsie and Jennie (Mol) Schut (mother), approximately 1920.
Left: Martin and Kathryn Dalman, Sylvia and Hazel (author's wife).
Below: Henry Schut.

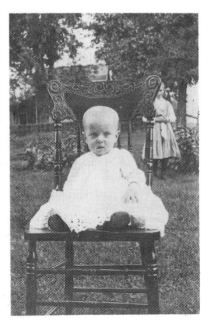

Above: Henry and Hazel Schut, taken on their wedding day, Sept. 9, 1935
Left: Silver Creek Reformed Church.

Above: Henry Schut and his 1927 Chevrolet Sedan.
Below: The author's two sons mowing the lawn. Wayne (pulling) Lawrence (pushing)

Right: In Ben Schneider's woods, one mile south of Roy Plaggerman's. Left to right — first two unknown, Albert Rozenberg, Wilmina Schut, Wilbert Schut and Elsie Schut.

Below: Henry Schut on right, with brother Bill and son Lawrence.

Henry Schut, cousin Harold Schut and cousin Jim Schut, taken in December 1933 at Grandpa's the winter Henry went to college.

Above: The author's family — front row, Marilyn, Linda, Lois and Darlene; back row, Lawrence, Henry, Hazel and Wayne.

Right: The author's six children — twins Lois and Linda, Wayne and Lawrence, Darlene and Marilyn.

Above: Son Lawrence on the farm.
Below: The new barn, built in 1952.

Above: District 16 Silver Creek School, 1917-18.
Right: Author's farm during his early life.
Below: Early view of Annandale High School when student buses had honest horse power. The author rode on one of these in 1932-33, boarding at Henry Larson's 1/2 mile east of town.

(photo courtesy of Pioneer Park, Annandale)

Above: Neighborhood threshing, taken in 1940.
Left: Henry Schut cutting cane for silage on a Massey Harris 81 tractor, taken in October 1942.
Below: Farming with horses in front of the original barn.

Above: Author's graduation at age 54 in 1964.
Right: Henry in the milk house of the new barn.

10

Grandpa (Martin) Dalman's Memory Lane

This chapter is a record of Hazel's father's memories of his youth as I interviewed him in the summer of about 1973 or 1974 when he stayed in our home after his gall bladder surgery. He was 88 or 89 years old. He had told me about many of these incidents before and I felt that these memories should be permanently recorded for posterity, so I taped the following interview which I have written down exactly as he spoke, except for a few remarks that I make for the sake of clarity. These I put in brackets. My questions to him are indicated as mine. (Note: The first part includes memories of what he was told of events that occurred when he was only one year old.)

Henry Grandpa [a title I called him though he was actually my father-in-law], when did you leave Michigan?
Martin I can't remember what village I was born in, but I do know it was in Michigan. It was on April 23, 1884. When I was a year old, that must have been in 1885, my folks and all, that is my father, my mother and all her sisters and brothers, they decided to go to [South] Dakota and homestead. They had bought covered wagons and rented a couple of cars for their furniture and their stock.
Henry The cars, you mean railroad cars, don't you?

121

Martin Ya, and then they went to Ipswich [S.D.]. They couldn't go any farther, as that was the end of the railroad.

Henry How far was that from where they homesteaded, do you know?

Martin I'm not sure how far that was; it was quite a bit farther than Eureka, which was 25 miles. But there was no railroad in Eureka yet and I'm sure the end of the road was Ipswich. Then they hooked up there and put their tents on there, then all traveled to their homestead from Ipswich.

Henry Do you know how many families went at this time? You said the Vork family; which other ones?

Martin I don't know if there were any other neighbors that came in the same bunch. But Uncle John Vork's wife was on the same train where he was, and they weren't married yet. They got married in Dakota later.

Henry Now tell us, how did they homestead? You said that they could get three quarter-sections [160 acres each]. Now how was that done?

Martin They took 160-acre homestead, then they could take a timber claim they could have, but they had to plant trees on it, so the government sent them trees. All these cottonwood sticks, about a foot long, came in bundles. The government furnished them, but the timber claim owner, he had to plant them, so we planted those little sticks but very few of them lived, 'cause it was dry and no loose soil, the sod was tough after you turned it over. Some of them lived, and some [people] had pretty good windbreaks out of them, but my folks never had any of them get started, I don't think. Then a [homesteader] could have another 160 acres, called a preemption, so you see they could get three quarters of land [480 acres].

Henry Just for moving out there?

Martin Then they had to stay on there, I think it was a year and one-half.

Henry And then it was theirs?

Martin Yes, then they could get their deed. That is what they called "prove up on it" when they got their deed. Then, you see, they could borrow money on it if they wanted to make [get] a loan on it. The times were tough and there was no money in the country.

Henry When they got there, there were no buildings, so how and where did they live?

Martin Of course, I was too young to remember. I don't know if they ever told me exactly what they did. But I have an idea they stayed in their covered wagons, then everybody got together and they must have had a plow which they took along from Michigan as there were no dealers around there anywhere, so they plowed the sod and they all got together with the wagons and they loaded up these pieces of sod and piled the sod up. It didn't take much over a day and they had a house ready, and they had all the walls done.

Henry How thick were these walls?

Martin These walls were about two feet thick. They cut the sod and I think the plow was 14 inches wide, then they cut 28-inch lengths, then laid them crossways. Then they would lay the next row lengthways to the wall [two pieces side by side]. That would bind the pieces of sod together. Then they went to the river and got cottonwood poles. They had to take their axe and cut them and peel the bark off. They laid one pole of about six or eight inches in diameter, from peak to peak [the end walls were built higher and tapered to a peak]. From that they had smaller poles, what they called rafters. They laid the bottom end of these poles on the side walls and the other end on top of what they called the ridge pole. Then they went back to the river to get some what they called diamond willow. You know, these were some of the prettiest willow you ever saw to make walking canes from.

Henry Is that right?

Martin Oh, them diamonds stood right out, high, you'd trim them off and if you varnished them, they were the prettiest canes you ever saw. Then they would put a little ring on the end; I don't exactly know how they did that. Of course you couldn't curve the ends.

Henry Then the canes were used just that way?

Martin Some had knobs on the top end, and that is just the way they used them. They were more for ornaments than anything else. [These were the same willows] they used to put on the roofs. They would lay them across those rafters, then when they had the brush all on they would go to work to get another load of sod and lay a layer of sod on top of those willows, and that was a pretty smooth roof. Then they went to a little low place, in what they called a gumbo flat—there are a lot of them in Dakota—then they would take that gumbo, a kind of yellow sticky stuff, and shovel that up. I think they plowed it loose first. They spread that all over that roof, right over the sod. They would put on a couple of inches, they would spread it out as even as they could. As soon as it started raining it would drip through a little because the clay wasn't stuck together yet in one cake, but after a few rains it would soften up and seemed to melt together in one piece. Then those roofs were just as nice and leak-proof and it never rained through at all. The [window and door] frames they must have taken along from Michigan in the [railroad] car. There was no place in that part of Dakota where you could buy any of those things, no lumber yards, no telephones. All there was, was a store in Thule, South Dakota. They fitted the windows and doors into the sod walls.

Henry Did the houses have more than one room?

Martin Well, they didn't make a partition out of the sod. Some of them put cheesecloth for a partition. They would whitewash that. It made a pretty good wall, and there wasn't any lumber to support it. I don't remember that there were any boards in there.

Henry It just hung from the roof then?

Martin Ya, some people covered the side walls with this cheesecloth and whitewashed them, some smoothened the walls and then plastered them with this yellow clay. Some also plastered them on the outside too [with the same clay]. That really made a pretty good-looking building, and cool, you never saw a building any cooler; the sun couldn't get through, it was cool in there all day. I think my folks and I lived in there for awhile before they had a floor in there. It was just a hard, dry, ground floor. If you swept it was kind of dusty. I guess at times they sprinkled it a little bit so they wouldn't have so much dust.

Henry Did they have a chimney in the house? How did they heat the house in the winter?

Martin No, that I can't tell for sure. I think they had just a stovepipe through the roof. I don't know how they prevented fire. Of course the sod and clay wouldn't burn. They probably pushed the brush aside a little and sealed in the stovepipe with clay. Inside the house they didn't have no heaters; some used straw burners.

Henry You said there wasn't anything to burn. What did you use?

Martin Well, there wasn't any coal, I don't remember when I was a kid that there was any coal till later. But they used hay, they had these burners, something like a wash boiler [an oblong type of kettle about 18 inches high with a capacity of 10 or 15 gallons], a kind of tank and they would go out to the haystack and pack it full of that hay, then took the cover of the cookstove, and turned this tank bottom-side up over the stove, and that fire would burn from that hay. The smoke would go right out through the stove, up the stovepipe. There was no smoke in the house.

Henry There must have been a good draft?

Martin Yes, there was a good draft. Then they discovered that they could use cow chips, the country was so dry, and the cow manure would lay in the pasture, just the way it came from the cow, heh, heh.

Henry I know they used to use buffalo dung like that.

Martin Ya. Then just as quick as the sky looked like rain, my mother would say, "Kids, hurry up. Go to the pasture and get some cow chips, 'cause it's going to rain." So we'd hurry down to the pasture with a couple of little home-made wagons and fill them with cow chips and put them in a box behind the stove. Some people used straw, but of course they had to raise a crop first before they had any straw, so they could not have had any straw till fall, because I think they moved out there in the spring, because they had to build their houses before fall. After they finished their houses, they started building barns, that was the same thing.

Henry All out of sod?

Martin Yes, there were no gutters [for the cows], just a dirt floor. The cows just stood in there. Most of the time they had enough straw and they could keep that pretty dry as the ground absorbed the moisture. And they used the same thing in the pig house. They had a pig house nearly as big as the barn.

Henry What did they do with the milk, how did they market it?

Martin Well, they dug a hole in the ground, what they called a dugout. They put a roof on that like they did on the house—poles, willows and sod. They had a trap door arrangement with steps down into the dugout. They kept their milk in there, and strained their milk into these flat pans. It would stand there for a day, when they would skim the cream off. When the cream was sour and they had enough, they would churn it with what they called a dash churn [a five to ten gallon barrel with a loose cover]. This cover had a hole in the middle through which a round broomstick handle was fitted. At the end of this handle they fastened a round board smaller in diameter than the barrel. By dashing this handle and stick up and down in the cream, the butter could be

126

separated from the cream.] Then they would make their own butter.

Henry Did they have some to sell too?

Martin Yes, they would put salt in there—my mother used to make real nice good butter. But the price was so low when they started selling this butter. They could take it to Thule, to Albert Van Dyke who ran the store there and they would trade it for groceries. The butter was only about 10 cents per pound at first, and eggs about a nickel per dozen, so the prices were really tough. I remember they were so short of money that they took corn—they could raise pretty fair corn—they used that squaw corn the Indians had raised there and the folks got some seed from them and called it squaw corn—it was short—they dried the corn, took a hammer and pounded it till it was cracked fine like coffee grounds, then they baked it in an oven till it got nearly black and that's what they used to make coffee. They couldn't afford to buy coffee even though it was only 10 cents a pound. I remember well they had Arbuckle coffee, 4X coffee, but they only bought that for company or special occasions, but for themselves they would drink that "corn juice." It tasted something like coffee though. I don't know how long they used it, because I was so young I can't remember exactly, but I know this all happened.

Henry You were telling me about the clothes. Can you tell us about that?

Martin Oh ya, we couldn't afford much clothes, but they built a church, which was made of sod too. This was built in the corner of my father's farm. I think it was either the first or second year we were there. Then the churches in the east who knew about this settlement, about the hard-up people, they used to send big boxes of used clothing that they collected for us. Then the elders and deacons of the church would open these boxes, they would take the clothes, shoes, coats, stockings, anything that the people could use. But too often they came home with a pair of shoes, they wouldn't fit us. We'd wear them anyway and then we would ruin our toes.

Henry You were telling me there were times that you didn't have shoes, even in the wintertime?

Martin Yes, sometimes we didn't wear shoes. We would keep those we had just for Sunday. On the weekdays they would take these grain sacks, cut pieces out of that, and sew them around our stockings. We did have stockings. We would walk right out in the snow and dig dirt with them. That was what we wore most of the time during the winter months. Of course in the summer we went barefooted. It was cheaper.

Henry Yes, I remember we did that too.

Martin Like Plaggermans, they were just as hard up as we were. I know none of us had very many shoes until we had been there quite a few years. After we got a few poor crops they could buy a little stuff. They couldn't buy much because the country was dry and they had so little machinery. I remember my father would go out, get the breaking [plowing] done. They would use oxen to do the breaking, they could work cheaper than horses, they could work without grain and horses can't hardly do that. Most of the settlers had oxen. They plowed with them. When they got quite a bit plowed then my father would go out there with a pail and a few sacks [of wheat] on the wagon. He would start early in the morning before the wind would start up, carry that pail of wheat under his arm, and he would spread that wheat by hand, up and down the field. Then they had a spike-toothed harrow, it didn't amount to nothing for those tough sods, they didn't make much impression. Well, about the only wheat that came up was from the seed that fell in the cracks between the sods, as they had a little more dirt underneath where it could take root. Some years they had a pretty fair crop. Some years we would have a good crop and we would get a hailstorm and that was the end of it.

128

Henry What did you do for excitement when you were all alone out on the prairie? Tell us about that.

Martin Well, it seems all the excitement we had, we went visiting our cousins, like the Plaggermans. They had kids about the same age. We would go down there and they would come to our house. We had little wagons, we had to make them ourselves. We would take a cottonwood pole, saw a round ring out of it. We didn't have a bit and brace [to drill a hole] so we took a nail, drove it through the center, then whittled around the nail hole until we had a fairly large hole through the ring. The rings were only about six or seven inches [in diameter] as that was the biggest pole we could find. Then we'd get a piece of wood, whittle the ends down, and put the wheels on that, put a nail through the ends, put a little grease on and we had a pretty good wagon. We used some old boards for a box to place on the axles. We had more fun making it than playing with it.

Henry You were telling me once about what you did when you got together with the cousins, the Cooks and Plaggermans. Tell us about that.

Martin Oh ya, that was the time my Aunt Priscilla got married. She married a man who came from Michigan. A lot of Dutchmen came in there to get a free homestead. They figured that three quarters of land was great. My father stayed there for 11 years. They had only a few crops that were fairly good, and the price was low, and then they had to haul this wheat. I don't know if they ever hauled it way to Ipswich, because the second or third year we were there the railroad came through Ipswich to Eureka, which was still 25 miles from our place. Then they would load up this wheat and haul it all the way to Eureka, and they had to stay there overnight, put the horses in the barn, and sleep in the hay in the livery barn. I don't know if they took their lunches along or if there were hotels there—I don't remember—I think they took most of their eats along. I think they got pretty dry again before they got home.

129

Henry You were telling me about the time they took some calves out of the barn.

Martin Oh ya, that was the time Aunt Priscilla got married. They tried everything to make a little fun. There was Uncle Eibert Cook and Uncle Dick Vork. They were quite a joke. They were the two worst ones. They went to the barn and they got a couple calves and turned them loose in the house. The women weren't used to working with those calves and were scared of those calves. The calves got wild in the house, they started running from one corner to the other, the women were all standing on chairs before they got the calves under control. Ha ha. Cook, of course, laughed his head off. Then they played games like "Blind Man's Bluff." I don't remember exactly how they played that. Then they played "Chook, Chook"—they'd all get on the floor in a big circle, with their knees up. They would get a cap and pass it from one to the other under their knees. There was a guy in the center, he had to find that cap; if he got hold of that cap he could get out of the center and the guy who he took it from would then be in the center. Every time the guy had his back turned, they would hit him on the seat with the cap. I don't know how long that cap lasted with that kind of treatment.

Henry How did you harvest the grain at that time?

Martin They didn't use a binder, because the grain was so short they couldn't catch it with the binder to make a bundle, so they had what they called headers. That was a machine with a carrier something like a binder with a reel but it was hooked up ahead of the horses, like a pole on a trailer. They would back that up with the sickle in front, with the reel over the sickle. The reel would throw the wheat heads on the canvas, which moved it to the elevator, which would elevate that into a header box. The box was built on the wagon and was made out of boards. The low side was about two feet high, the other side was about five feet high. Us kids used to have to go in that box and drive the horses. One guy would stand on the

back of the header, there was a steering pole behind the
header, he would stand on the support beam with the steering
pole between his legs, he could steer the header in any
direction he wished to go. On the end he would turn the
header around and the horses would just follow. They were
tied there and didn't need to be driven. Sometimes on the
ends of the field the horses would have to be steered so they
could turn shorter.

Henry Then it was one of the first self-propelled machines
because it cut ahead of the power [of the horses as they went].

Martin Ya, when the box was full, they took the heads—they
had two boxes—they would drive it and unload it and make a
stack. It was all loose stuff, all short grain. It was heavy stuff.
The stacks were about 10 by 14 feet. They didn't make them
very high, but rounded them on the top, then made another
one. Sometimes they had a lot of stacks. They didn't put the
stacks all in one place as the fields were a half-mile long if
they went clear across the homestead, so they put stacks on
both ends and when the threshing machine came they would
move from one setting to the other. Sometimes they had a fair
crop, but the trouble was that part where we lived was the dry
part of Dakota. It was right on the north edge of South
Dakota. Farther north there was a Holland settlement there—I
don't know when they settled there—it was called Westfield.
There they had better land and seemed to get more rain.
Those farmers became well off. They had a lot of land and
got good crops. I saw some fellow buy 160 acres and put 100
acres into flax the very first crop. They had those big tractors
called oil pull—they pulled four, six or eight plows.

Henry Did they have them at that time already?

Martin No, I guess not the first time I was there, that came
later. I got ahead of my story. At first we had oxen and
horses. But horses couldn't do much with a breaking
plow—that buffalo sod was tough. It took two good-sized
oxen to pull them plows—they handled it good. They didn't

walk as fast as horses but they had the strength. The trouble was, if they would have had a good disk or sprint-tooth harrow, they could have worked up the sod a lot better right away the first year and more of that grain would have gotten roots, because a lot of the seeded grain laid on top of the sod and didn't sprout. It laid there in the sun and got burned so they didn't get a very good stand. But later on when it was plowed the second time it broke up better, and pretty soon they got some loose dirt. But the trouble was, there was never enough rain, and the soil where we were was pretty light. That was about two and a half miles northwest of where Herreid stands today. But when we were there Herreid wasn't there yet and Pollock, South Dakota, wasn't there either. The nearest town was Mound City and that was 10 miles south of us. That is where we went mostly for our trading. In Thule you couldn't buy much. They had a post office and a store where you bought groceries and some shoes.

Henry Now I'd like to have you tell me about the Indian scare.

Martin Ya, after we lived there a few years, I think I was around six. One night we were in the house eating supper—it was about twilight—my uncle Eibert Cook came on horseback to the house. He didn't even get off the horse, he just yelled "Gerrit!" (that's my father's name) "Gerrit, turn everything loose you got and head for Eureka—the Indians are coming!" Everybody got excited, we went out and turned the cows loose, all the pigs loose. We had quite a few pigs by then too, because we had been able to raise some corn to feed them. So we turned all the stuff loose and away we went to Eureka. It was just about getting dark, we all sat in the wagon, I guess Pa had a spring seat on the front where he sat to drive. But the whole family, all of us kids, were sitting in the back of the wagon. How we could stand those bumps, I don't know. There was rocks and bumps of grass, and hardly any trail. It was all we could do to follow the trail, and this was in the night. We were on the road all night long. We got to Eureka about morning, everybody was milling around. The whole town was full of people, everybody was trying to get away from the Indians. Some were so scared, they took the train and went back to Michigan.

Henry They never came back to stay?

Martin No, my uncle Henry Moss, my Aunt Dora, they got so scared, they got on the train and went back to Michigan, but later though they came back. I think we stayed in Eureka about three days. Everybody was talking about the Indians, but nobody knew what really happened. Some said the Indians were swimming across the Missouri River on their horses. It was just about the same time they had a fight there, and it was about that time that Chief Sitting Bull was killed. They had had a fight with the soldiers that were there, that was on the west side of the river, that was called the Standing Rock Reservation. Those few Indians, they were tough, a whole lot worse than those Indians we have here in Minnesota now.

Henry Yes, but they were angry for a reason.

Martin Ya, of course, they were mad because the government took the land away from them and pushed them back across the Missouri River and that was why they had so much trouble with the Indians. You couldn't hardly blame them.

Henry No, you really couldn't.

Martin One night—this happened already before the Indian scare—they came across the river—I don't know how they crossed the river—there were some people who lived only maybe a mile or two from the river. A man and a woman had a daughter and son-in-law. They were together one evening, they may have been living with each other, I don't know. Anyway, the women were in the house, this was just after supper, the men were in the barn doing the chores and here come the Indians. I don't know how many there was in the bunch. They went to the barn first and killed the men and then went to the house and killed the women. That was what they called the Spicer family.

Henry Now getting back to your story. How long did you stay in Eureka?

Martin We stayed about three days and nothing seemed to happen. There were a bunch of boys, they were all good [horse] riders, you might call them cowboys. A bunch of these got on their horses and they rode back to see. I suppose if they did run into the Indians they could turn back and outrun them maybe. So they picked out some pretty good guys and they went back [to the homestead] to look, so I guess they went all the way back to Lagrace, that was a little place on this side of the river, just a store there and I don't know what else. Anyway, they found out it was a false report, the Indians never got across the river. Somebody started a false report. So they came back and said they thought it was perfectly safe. So everybody started moving back slowly on. Some of them were a little skeptical, but the most of them, it didn't take too long, they moved back again and everything went on again as usual. We didn't hear no more about the Indians. That one family, of course, had been killed earlier.

Henry Do you remember if you found all your pigs, cows and horses again?

Martin Ya, nothing happened. They were still around the yard, there was no place to go to, near as I can remember. The cows and pigs were soon back in their places. I don't remember exactly what time of the year it was. It wasn't winter, I know, because the weather was warm. There was one big joke that happened [during this time] when Uncle Eibert got through notifying all these farmers [about the Indians coming]. He sent his wife, Aunt Minnie and the kids, I think they had about three kids then, he had sent her with the horse and buggy to go to Eureka. When finally Uncle Eibert got through notifying all the people, he headed for Eureka too. He was looking for Aunt Minnie of course. He drove along on the horse, pretty soon my Aunt Minnie happened to look back and saw a guy coming behind her on horseback. It was kinda dark and she couldn't tell what or who it was. When she saw it was a guy, she thought it was an Indian, and she stepped on those horses, she went so fast with those horses and buggy, Uncle Eibert had quite a "tussle" to catch up with her. He finally caught up with her and yelled at her, "I'm your husband!"

Henry Seems rather funny, but really wasn't, for them to be racing each other.
Martin Ya, it seemed funny. I would have done the same thing if I had looked back and saw someone coming on horseback. I would have tried to get away too.
Henry You mentioned some things that happened later.
Martin Ya, quite a few years later when Pa and all the Vorks went to Minnesota, they got tired of all that country, it was always too dry. The last year they were there, they had a fair crop, but wheat was only 38 cents per bushel. They could hardly afford to haul it for 25 miles to Eureka and get only 38 cents. They didn't make nothing at that. So they got tired of it, and they just picked up and a bunch of them went in the spring with covered wagons. That was Uncle Johnie, Uncle Albert, Uncle Dick, Uncle Peter and two of the girls of Uncle Albert, they were young girls then. They didn't want too many to go on the train. That would cost more money.
Henry These uncles were all Vorks, weren't they?
Martin Ya, they traveled all the way from that country what they called Thule, where we were in Campbell County. They traveled all the way to Minnesota with the wagon, but my father and my grandfather [Vork] went to Minnesota the year before and looked over this land, and that was right after this Hinckley fire, because it was pretty well burned off; otherwise they could not have settled there, as there was thick, heavy timber, with pine trees up to 200 feet long. But after the fire,

that opened up the country, then, you see, you could go in there. There wasn't hardly anything left but the stumps and a lot of these logs were laying there. So they each bought 80 acres. My father and my grandfather [Vork] and they came back from Minnesota. Then in the fall they got a couple of boxcars [railroad cars]. They put the cattle and the machinery, what they wanted to take along, and they traveled with the boxcar, and they landed in what they called Groningen [Minnesota]. I can't tell you exactly where we lived, but this land agent that was selling all this land in Pine County, his name was Koff. He was a big land man from St. Paul, and he had a building in Groningen that he built so that people who came in could move in there for a time until they got a house built. It was a nice big building, there were three big rooms. Later, they used one of these rooms for a schoolhouse. There is where I went to school.

Henry That was near Sandstone or Hinckley, wasn't it?

Martin No, that was 15 miles west of Sandstone. In the middle room of that house [in Groningen], the storekeeper was living in there [later]. I happened to work for this man. He was running a sort of livery business from Groningen to Sandstone. He had a nice little team of sorrel horses, and he was hauling these men. These men had no way to travel. They would come on the freight train or passenger train, but you could see they couldn't stop as many times as they wanted to, so they would land in Sandstone and they would come across to Groningen, these salesmen. [The owner of the livery stable] would haul them wherever they wanted to go. I was only a young kid, I think I must have been about 14, because it happened before we got struck by that lightning [his brother Albert was killed by lightning], and I was working in that store, and his wife and he lived in that middle part of that building. I worked for that fellow about all winter. I took care of the store and the post office—he had the post office in there too. The depot agent would pick up the mail that came in on the flyer, on the N.P. (Northern Pacific). He would bring the mail by bag to the post office and I would open it with the key, and I would sort the mail and put it in boxes, or give it to the farmers when they came in for their mail. I also worked by Lake Levin, cooking for 16 men. I used to be my mother's hired girl, because there was boys and there was no girls yet, so she made a girl out of me, and I learned to do everything in the house. I'd get up in the morning, bake cornbread, get the table ready. My mother would stay in bed with [my sister] Alice, she was a baby. Pa was in Michigan, visiting there for the winter—I don't know how long he stayed—[This happened when the family lived in Dakota] maybe a month or six weeks, I know he made quite a story. Alice would have the colic at night and Ma would walk the floor at night and wouldn't get much sleep. So in the morning, Alice would fall asleep and so did my mother. I'd get up and bake the cornbread and get the breakfast ready. You see, Ralph and Jake were older than I and they went to the barn to do the chores, feed the cows and do whatever there was to do.

Henry Now let us take another look at your life in North Dakota. When did you go back with Uncle Jake Dalman and take this homestead claim?

Martin Oh ya, when I was older, brother Jake went to Dakota on a homestead. I can't remember what year that was, but Bert Meintsma and I decided we wanted to see Jake and his wife, Ezetta. Bert and I got together. I had a horse and buggy there, because I had been out there working in the summer. In the winter, I left the horse and buggy there and came to Minnesota. [The Dalman family had moved from Groningen to Maple Lake and the date must have been around 1904.] In the spring Bert Meintsma wanted to see Jake so he said, "Why don't we go to see Jake on the homestead there." That was way across the reservation on the other side of Lemmon, South Dakota. When Jake moved down to the homestead there was no railroad in Scranton, North Dakota. And they settled

10 miles south of Scranton. But when they settled there, the town wasn't there yet and no railroad there either. But they took the train to Dickenson. Jake's father-in-law went along with him and his wife and Harry, their son. They took a team of mules along on the boxcar and unloaded their stuff at Dickenson, North Dakota, and then from there south to the homestead. That was 75 miles, and filed on these homestead, on adjoining 160 acres of land.

Henry How did you get involved out there, did you take a claim out there then?

Martin I believe I did, I think Jake told me when I got down there, "I don't know of any 160"—you see I wanted to settle close to Jake because I didn't want to be way out there alone somewhere—I was still single. Jake said, "There's an 80 acres cornering my place, you can still get that for a homestead." So I went over and looked at it, and thought, well, 80 acres is better than nothing! So I filed on that 80 acres, and I sold the horse and buggy out there somewhere and went back on the train to Westfield. Bert Meintsma went back [to Minnesota] and I went back to carpenter work all summer, then in fall—you had six months to move on your claim or you would lose it—[just before] the time was up, I went back to my homestead. I bought some stuff in Westfield. I bought four wild steers who never had a rope on. They weighed about 1200 pounds a piece. I think I paid $50 each for the steers. So we put them in a [box] car and I bought a yoke—an old yoke from an old Hollander in Westfield. He had horses by that time but he still had the old yoke. I also had a pony that I could ride, and I put that in the car too. Then when we went to the homestead, by that time the railroad was through to Scranton, North Dakota, so I had only 10 miles to go. Brother Jake had to go 75 miles [when he went]. So we unloaded the steers. I'm not sure how we got the steers home. I think I drove them with the pony, because you couldn't lead them, because you couldn't get a rope on them. Well, I got the steers home to Jake's place—he had a fence by the barn—we got the steers into the fence by the barn. Then we bought some rings to put into their nose. Somehow we got them in, even though they were scared of us. We did put a ring in their nose so we could lead them, that's the only way we could handle them.

Henry Tell us how you broke them.

Martin There was a corner fence past by the barn, we took two of them steers, and tied them to the fence past [the barn] and then we put the yokes on them, and pulled the wagon up behind them and hooked it onto the yoke. Of course, everything had to be tied down because the oxen got so scared. Then we tied the box to the wagon, else it would bounce off. There was nothing but prairie out there and no road around anywhere. Jake got into the wagon and stood in the box, hanging onto a cross rope that was tied down over the top of the box, and I got the pony. I took the oxen and untied them and got them away from that post and left them go. There Jake was in that box, and that wagon was bouncing over those rough bumps of buffalo grass. I rode the pony and kept guiding those oxen around and around over the prairie. We kept it up until the oxen were completely tired out, then we could lead them home slowly. The next day we did the same thing again until in about two weeks we could hook them up and they would be just as tame, and we could tame them to obey by using the words "Gee" and "Haw" for turning and "Whoa" and "Giddap" for stopping and going.

This ended the interview. He told me he didn't stay on the homestead very long, as a year or two later when they had a good wheat crop, all in stacks, a prairie fire destroyed his whole crop. He then returned to Westfield and became a carpenter.

Martin Dalman died on December 12, 1979.

His first wife, Cathrine (Katie), died July 4, 1915.

Their children were Hazel (born 1912) and Sylvia (1914). At the time of this writing they are both still living.

His second wife, Agnes, died in 1957. Their children were Mildred (1921-1975), Vernon (1922—), Harvey (1924—), Harold (1926—), Kenneth (1928-1983), and Lester (1931—).

11

Our Wedding, 1935

Weddings reflect many of the social values and customs of the times. Ours was quite typical of the 1930s and perhaps of 10 or 20 years before that.

A bride's parents were normally expected to provide her wedding, but as Hazel's mother was no longer living and Hazel was living with her aunt and uncle, Ella Mae and Jake Mol, it was they who gave it for her, with some help from other relatives and part of the money Hazel had saved. The wedding took place at 11 a.m., September 4, 1935, in Silver Creek Reformed Church. The church was then located about three and a half miles north of Maple Lake. My brother Bert and Hazel's sister Sylvia were the only attendants. The ceremony was a very simple one with many from our church group present.

A special dinner for the older relatives and friends was served at Jake Mol's home after the wedding. Our afternoon was spent visiting and preparing for the young people's reception in the evening. The food was all prepared and served by invited volunteers. There was no problem in obtaining volunteers to serve at weddings, since it was considered an honor to be asked. Besides, the volunteers enjoyed the excitement.

When evening came, the young people, our peer group, and friends and relatives who had been invited joined us to help celebrate. The chairs were carried out or placed in a corner of the room. Some of our musical friends played harmonicas and accordions while the rest of us played "square skip." That was similar to square dancing. We also enjoyed several party or parlor games. One I remember was called "Pig in the Parlor."

A sudden, earsplitting noise came from outside the door about 9 p.m. It was a "shivaree" bunch. I had been expecting them because nearly every wedding had these uninvited guests. They began by banging on buzz saws, cowbells, disk blades and anything that would produce noise. The clatter would continue until the bride and bridegroom made their appearance outside the door. Then the appointed leader would congratulate the couple and "solicit" a cash gift so the shivaree group could celebrate on their own—at the expense of the groom. As I had been the leader at many similar occasions, I knew it was customary not to yield to the first request. This would then give the whole group cause to increase their noise-making until the bridegroom finally agreed to negotiate with the leader. I paid them five dollars, which was ample at that time for each of them to get a treat. Sometimes they would hold a party a couple of weeks later and invite the newlyweds as special guests.

There were some weddings where shivarees were definitely not welcome. In that case, the group would begin to vandalize the place and threaten the bride and groom if no money were forthcoming. However, these were in the minority.

After our shivaree group left, we returned to the party games. We served no alcoholic beverages, but there were probably some guests who brought their own. In our time and in our church group that was frowned upon. A late lunch was served from 11 to 12 p.m. after which some guests went home. Most of them stayed on into the wee hours.

Hazel and I stayed at the home of Uncle Jake that night, and, true to our religious upbringing, we slept together for the first time. It was a short night because we had to help clean up in the morning and take back the numerous things that had been borrowed from neighbors for the wedding.

As it was silo-filling time and we had no money for a honeymoon, I filled silo the next day at a neighbor's farm. At least, that meant I could get help to fill ours.

I had brought my bride back home with me. She and I had one room and a kitchen upstairs in the old farm house. Mother, John, and Bill lived in the rest of the house. We had no electricity or water in the house, no bathroom, no furnace and no bed. Hazel still had $125 from her work with which we bought a gasoline range, a table and chairs, and some cooking utensils. She had bought a dresser earlier and had received a folding cot from a Mrs. Moore, one of her employers in the city. It could be made into a couch during the day and a bed at night. With a linoleum rug on the floor, curtains at the window, and a colorful cover for the couch, we felt that we had very nice living quarters.

Any water for cooking, washing dishes, or washing face and hands had to be carried upstairs. Then the waste water had to be carried back down again to be discarded outside. On the other hand, we had no sewer problems, no fuses to burn out, no water pipes to freeze up nor many of the other problems of today.

We did have to buy kerosene for our lamps, trim their wicks, polish their sooted glass chimneys, cut wood for the old stove in our room and carry out the ashes nearly every day. We also had to thaw out that outside pump in the winter and do a host of other things we would like to forget.

In spite of or maybe because of these inconveniences we were very happy. We are living proof that happiness is not dependent on a beautiful home or on new furniture. Hazel had a special knack of making even the most humble surroundings look bright and cheerful. Her handiwork and neatness were constant reminders of how she made each dollar we spent do triple duty.

12

A Summer Day on the Farm, 1936

"Jangle, jangle," goes the old mechanical alarm clock.
From the nearby bed I moan and reach out to shut it off
with a heavy slap. How could those clock hands have whirled
away seven hours so quickly?

No time to yawn. No time to stretch. Gotta get out of these
pajamas, into a pair of B.V.D.s (undershorts, that is). Then a
blue chambray shirt, a blue denim bib overall, some Rockford
socks and a pair of eight-inch leather shoes. Now, out the
door.

Looks like a hot day coming up. The sun is barely up over
the horizon and it's already over 70 degrees. I walk to the
barn where Barney, Topsy, Jim and Old Bill welcome me with
whinnies as if to say, "Hey! It's time for breakfast. Where
have you been?"

A large share of this breakfast is up in the haymow. At Old
Bill's insistence, I climb the ladder through the trap door in
the mow floor, get the fork and throw four forkfuls of hay
down the hay chute. I follow, half tumbling, to the soft pile
below. I have been careful not to land on the fork,
remembering what its sharp teeth once did to my leg. I grab
the fork by its handle and pitch a forkful of hay at each horse.
I walk over to the grain bin. Oh, oh! Old Bill has been there
during the night and helped himself. I'm sure I put a turn
button on the door last night and tied his halter rope in a
double knot. But he really likes his oats, and even more, he
enjoys outwitting me.

A Summer Day on the Farm, 1936

A knot is just an inconvenience to him. If one is a bit
troublesome for his teeth to loosen, a couple rubs of his halter
buckle will make his halter drop off. Then he'll walk
nonchalantly to the grain bin, rub his lips on the turn button,
slip his nose under the wooden lid and, "upsy-daisy," the
feast is ready.

Most horses would eat till they were sick, but not Old Bill.
He knows better. As soon as he has had enough, he strides
back to his stall and stands there just as though nothing has
happened.

I look his way. Sure enough, the halter rope is dangling into
the manger. I feed a gallon measure of oats and two ears of
corn to each of the other three horses. When I walk beside Old
Bill to tie him up, he looks at my empty oats pail as if to say,
"I ain't hungry this morning, anyway."

The cows come next. I fill a bushel basket with a mixture of
ground oats and corn. A gallon or more goes in front of each
open stanchion. I take the basket back to the bin and fill a
small bucket with linseed oil meal from a sack along the wall.
I give a cupful to each cow but not to Susie. She's going dry
so she doesn't need the extra protein.

Going to the back door, I open it and yell, "Come, boss!
Come, boss!" The herd is lying in the pasture about a quarter
mile away. If the cows are hungry enough, they might come.
If not, I will have to walk after them. It'll take a kick in the
rump to get each of them up and moving so I can drive them
into the yard, then into the barn. Our dog Rex will run along
and nip a few heels too. We can be in the barn in a short time.
I hope desperately that it won't be necessary this morning.
There is a busy day ahead and I want to get started before it
gets too hot.

I go into the small milk house I built inside the barn. It
really doesn't deserve the name. It's only a cow stall with
three sides walled up with boards. It's about three by five feet
over all. No door. Just room for a shelf to hold the 14-quart

milk bucket and a strainer, and for two eight-gallon milk cans under it. The cream separator is bolted to the floor between the shelf and the opening that serves as a door. I assemble the cream separator and pull the two cans out from under the shelf, placing the milk strainer on one can and a cover on the other to keep out those ever-present, ever-hungry flies. I sure hope the cows are hungry this morning!

As I walk back to the door, I see I am lucky. The cows are all walking through the yard toward me. All except Susie. Being heavy with calf, she isn't interested in moving very fast. I don't especially care whether she comes or not. She can wait till evening to be milked. The first cow walks in and finds her place. I walk over and lock the stanchion around her neck. Seven more find their places, but Mabel has to be different. She sticks her head into Susie's stanchion. I walk in front of her, give her a poke in the nose with my foot and scold, "Get out of there, that's not your place, and you know it!" She backs out slowly and goes where she belongs, looking at me as if to ask, "Why are you so confounded particular? Every stanchion looks the same to me."

Susie hasn't arrived yet, but I pick up my milk stool and bucket and park myself under the first cow. With the bucket between my knees, I grab her front teats, one in each hand, and start milking. The first 10 or 20 squirts make a ringing sound when they hit the bottom of the bucket. Soon a foam rises and I hear only the smooth gurgle of warm milk hitting that already in the bucket. If only the cows would all milk like Spot! During the half minute it takes for her to "let down" her milk, she gives nearly a cupful with each squirt. Then the stuff nearly runs out by itself. Now I can plan some of my day's work. Whoops! The foam is running over the side. I'll have to empty the pail. Spot is being extra generous today. I pour the milk into the strainer and hear it entering the can. I return to strip out the last milk from her udder.

We had named the next two cows Hans and Fritz after the

familiar cartoon characters, the Katzenjammer Kids. I quickly milk Hans and start on Fritz. The milk in the bucket is just beginning to foam when Spot, the first cow I milked and the second one behind me, decides to urinate. Hans, the cow right behind me, swings that bushy end of her tail to the right, behind Spot. It is soaked like a mop when she swings it back and wraps it around my face. Yuk! I grab my bucket and stool, set them on the alley and sputter as I run the three rods past the barn door to the stock tank. I jerk the trap door open, stick both hands into the water, and douse my face several times. My neck, too. Clean water drips from my face and hands as I walk back into the barn. A rag that is hanging by the separator serves as a towel. Fritz, feeling abandoned, looks around at me as if to say, "Where'd you go so fast?"

"I'd like to tie your tail in two knots!" I mutter at Hans. (But then, what would she use for a fly swatter?)

Roughly, I unlatch the stanchions for the two trouble makers and growl, "Now get outside!"

Back to Fritz again, I finish up with her and move along. Finally, only Blackie is left. She has just freshened the day before with her first calf and is still a little wary of my intentions. It's a brand new experience for her. I talk soothingly to her as I take my bucket. "So, boss. So, boss. I'm not going to hurt you."

I place my left leg against her right hind one so she can't get a swing at me, then slowly reach down and massage her udder. This feels good to her and she starts to relax. I hold the bucket with one hand and slip the other one slowly to the teat nearest me. I rub it slowly and softly, then grasp it between my thumb and pointer, stripping downward. A squirt of rich yellow milk strikes the bottom of the pail.

The first milk from a newly freshened cow (one that has just had a calf) is called cholesterum. It has special nutrients that help the calf make the transition from life in the womb to life in the harsh outside world. Sometimes I let the calf suck the first day or two, but that makes it much more difficult to get the calf to learn to drink from a pail. Also, the mother develops an attachment to the calf and it is harder to "break" her for hand-milking.

A couple of times more and I feel Blackie relax. I set the bucket on the floor, reach back for another teat and begin stripping it. I grope cautiously for my stool and sit down. This is going to take time. These teats aren't much more than buttons on her stiff udder. It'll be weeks before I can milk her with a full hand. It takes 10 minutes to pull out a gallon of milk now.

Whoever coined the phrase "cows give milk" *sure* had never milked a heifer for its first time. I try to feed some of the milk to the calf, but am not very successful so decide to wait till evening.

I loosen the stanchion latch and Fritz backs out. She bolts out the door and I close it behind her. I notice Susie did finally make it to the barn. Her look seems to say, "Don't you want me to come in?"

I tell her, "Naw, you can wait till tonight."

I return to the 15 gallons of milk that are in the two cans and fill the supply tank on the separator with five gallons of the liquid, then start winding the hand crank up to about 48 rounds per minute. Through a series of gears, this spins the bowl over a thousand r.p.m. to separate the cream from the whole milk. Cream pours out of one spout into a can and skim milk out of the other into a large pail. It takes about 10 minutes to separate the 15 gallons. I take the skim milk out and pour it into the hog trough. The little pigs are climbing over each other, squealing, grunting, each trying to be first to get its snout in the warm drink. I count them as they line up on each side of the trough. By the time I get to 31, the milk has disappeared. They look up—"Is that all there is?"

I carry a basket to the corn crib, fill it, and dump the corn over the fence to the hogs. Now back to the barn again I place a cover on the can containing a gallon and a half of cream and put the can in a barrel of cold well water.

I'll need a milk bucket of water from the stock tank to rinse out the milk cans. It's out and back once more. I run some of it through the separator, which is still revolving, and take the rinse water to the hogs. Back to the barn for the last time to dismantle the separator and carry it and the milk cans to the house. Hazel will wash them during the day.

It is nearly 7 a.m. How I wanted to get out in the field by seven-thirty! I know it won't happen now. I walk into the house where Hazel has breakfast ready and put my arms around her waist, but she pushes me back. "Phew! What happened to you?"

"Oh! I forgot. I was given a shampoo by Hans this morning."

"You'd better have it redone if you want to get close to me. I don't think I want you to sit by the table with that *scent.*"

"Well, I'm hungry and I gotta eat, so I better get another shampoo."

"Yes, and use a bar of Palmolive soap this time. I don't care about the perfume in the shampoo you had this morning," she complains.

"Why not? That's what we call Lady Esther perfume."

"Smells more like Lady Cow to me," she replies.

I take the teakettle from the stove, pour a little warm water into the wash basin and rub my hair full of soap. I rinse the soap off with water from the cistern pump and dry off most of it with a towel.

"Now that should smell better," I tell Hazel.

She walks over, take a whiff, and gives me a big hug.

Breakfast looks good. It's always my favorite meal of the day. This morning there is a large bowl of cooked oatmeal, an egg and lots of home-baked bread with butter. I'm almost too hungry to ask God's blessing on the food, but I do. I'm done eating in minutes and we read a short portion of Scripture. We give thanks for our blessings and I'm out the door.

I'm halfway to the barn before I remember it's my turn to take the cream to the creamery in Silver Creek. Dykhuizens, our neighbors, took it in Monday, so today, Wednesday, is my turn. I wheel around to our old 1927 Chevrolet standing by the door. I get in, back up to the cooler by the stock tank, and pour this morning's cream into that from the day before. I pull the eight-gallon can out of the cooler, place it in front of the back seat, and wish we had a newer car. One with a trunk. But there is no money to buy it. Hazel calls from the house.

"We need some butter and flour. I think we are nearly out of chick feed, too."

"O.K. I'll pick up some," I promise.

I drive over to Dykhuizens where two cans of cream are ready to go. I load them into the back seat and start rolling for town. When I arrive at the creamery, I find only two other farmers ahead of me at the unloading ramp. Not bad, I must be ahead of the rush.

Less than five minutes later I'm lifting the cans out of the car and placing them on the unloading platform. Lawrence Clausen, the buttermaker, reaches through the small door, grabs the handle and pulls one of the cans toward him.

"Good morning!" he yells above the noise of the steamer. "You're early this morning. You aren't in a hurry, are you?"

"Yep," I inform him. "It's going to be hot and I want to get out in the cornfield before the sun gets too high."

"Where's your cream record book?" he asks. "There's a slip on the can for two pounds of butter, but no cream book."

"Oh, here it is." I pick it up from the ground and hand it to him. "It fell off when I lifted the can out of the car."

Lawrence pushes the hot steamed cans back through the door and hands me the butter. I drive to the feed house next door where the feed man loads up a sack of chick feed and a hundred pounds of flour. I sign the charge slip and I'm on my way back. I drop off Dykhuizens' empty cans on the way

151

home. It all took only 25 minutes, but it is nearly 8 a.m. I
wanted to be out in that cornfield before half past seven!

I unload the cream can by the barn, park the car by the
house and run for the barn. I'll need only two horses to pull
the cultivator and decide to take Old Bill and Jim. They are
older and know how to follow the corn rows without my
constant guidance.

I grab their collars from the hook on the wall and fasten
them around their necks. Then, my back to the wall, I thread
my right arm through the harness, grasp the harness and
hames and throw the harness on Jim's back. I must buckle all
the straps securely. There are hame straps to keep the hames
on the collar, two back-up straps to snap to the neck yoke
strap, and a heavy buckle on the belly band which goes
around the chest just behind the front legs. Now the bridle. I
hold the headpiece in my right hand and the bit in my left.
The bit goes between Jim's lips and I'm hoping he will open
his jaws to let the bit slide into his mouth. He knows what that
means so he's not about to cooperate. I pry his mouth open
with my fingers and with a little pressure on the bit, I get him
to accept it. After I buckle up his neck band, the entire routine
is gone through again for Old Bill.

Oops! I can't take them out yet. I nearly forgot to give
Topsy and Barney their drink. I walk across the alley, unfasten
their halter ropes, lead them to the stock tank where they drink
greedily, then it's back to their stalls to tie them up. I notice
that the water in the stock tank is low. The cows must have
drunk a considerable amount already. I walk over and put the
windmill in gear to pump the tank full again.

I lead Old Bill and Jim from the barn, let them drink and
hook them up to the cultivator. The rest is going to be easy
for me. There is a seat on the cultivator where I can sit while
guiding the two "gangs" as the horses pull them through the
ground. They have two sharp hoe-like shovels. I'll have to lift
these gangs at the end of each row so we can turn around, then

drop them again when we go to the next row, but that's not hard to do.

The first row takes the most time. The cultivator shovels have to be adjusted so they throw the soil exactly the right way and the depth has to be set just right. The shields that prevent the dirt from covering the corn have to be positioned to permit the right amount of dirt to cover the weeds but not the small corn. Also, the horses must be guided and paced. Too much speed will cover the corn. The second row goes better. The mark left by the shovels the first time will serve as a guide for the horses. Now Old Bill will follow the mark all the way across the field without any help from me.

By 10 a.m. it is already hot out there and the horses are sweating. They need a rest. I turn around on the end of the field nearest home and head for the house and a coffee break. I can trust Old Bill and Jim to stand right there even if it gets to be an hour, but I spend only 10 minutes and we continue our slow, tedious task.

At noon I drive the team and cultivator to the barn, unhitch the horses, give them a drink, feed them some hay and grain, then go into the house for dinner. The horses need a good hour to eat and rest so my dinner will be quite leisurely. A hearty meal of potatoes, meat, vegetable, and a fruit sauce is nearly ready when I come in the door. I pour some water into the basin and wash the dirt and sweat from my arms and face. I notice that the pail of waste water is full, so I carry it out behind the chicken house and dump it. The eight-gallon can of cooking and drinking water is nearly empty and the little water that is left is warm, so I take it to the pump, change the valve from the stock tank to the spout on the well and set the can under it.

The wind is blowing rather slowly and it will take the windmill some time to fill the can. I return to the house to eat. Right after dinner, I sprawl on the floor and take a five-minute snooze.

A Summer Day on the Farm, 1936

I wake up and go to the pump. The can of water is running over, so I shut off the valve. Seeing the stock tank is full enough, I shut off the windmill, then carry the can of water back to the house.

I take Old Bill and Jim out for another drink and hook them in front of the cultivator again. Because the afternoon is so hot, the horses must rest quite often. I have taken a hoe along and I try to stop the horses near a patch of thistles so I can hoe them off while the horses rest. At 3:30 I start watching for Hazel to bring coffee and lunch out to me. I look forward to that time because I enjoy sitting in the shade at the end of the field and visiting with her. Those 15 minutes pass swiftly and I go back to the cultivator. When 5:30 arrives, I drive a couple of tired horses to the barn. They don't need any coaxing to go home. They know very well that feed and water are waiting. I unhook them from the cultivator, take off their bridles and lead them by the halters to the stock tank. They both begin to drink greedily, but I pull them away for a moment or two. The water is cold and too much all at once can make them sick. Their thirst quenched, they walk into their stalls. I tie them up, pull off their harnesses and collars and brush both horses down with a curry comb and stiff brush. I pat them each on the neck, saying, "Good job today boys," and I give them their feed and hay. Old Bill has recovered his appetite since last night's clandestine raid on the oat bin.

I distribute grain in the cow manger, go to the house to get the separator and cans and prepare them for the evening's milking. From the barn door I see that the cows are in the yard, waiting. I walk to the gate and close it so they can't go back to the pasture before I'm ready to milk. The pigs are already squealing, so I give them their corn and some water, but— "Where is that yummy milk?"

"You are going to have to wait an hour or so," I tell them. As I walk to the house for supper, Hazel is just putting the

finishing touches to it. By 6:30 I'm busy milking. I finish
within an hour, then separate the milk. Now I have to try
feeding that stubborn new calf of Blackie's. He didn't drink
much in the morning, so perhaps tonight he'll be more
cooperative. I take a small bucket with about three quarts of
his mother's milk in it, straddle my legs over the calf and back
him into the corner. I stick the pail under his nose, but nature
tells him that milk is supposed to come from above, so his
nose goes up in the air. I stick two fingers into this mouth and
he starts to suck. With all the force I can muster, I bend his
neck so his head goes down into the bucket.

"Well, that tastes good, but how come it's down there?"

I pull my fingers out, hoping he will continue to drink. But
no, up comes the head again and we start the process all over.
I try a couple more times. Finally, I take the palm of my hand
on the top of his head and force his nose into the milk. He
takes a couple of sips, gives the side of the pail a terrific bump
from inside and sends it sailing across the pen. Milk spills over
the straw, onto my shoes, down my overall and up my sleeve
all at the same time. I tell him, "That's all for tonight! Maybe
tomorrow morning you'll have more sense."

I wash the sticky milk off as best I can in the stock tank,
open the pasture gate for the cows, feed the skim milk to the
hogs and little pigs as I had promised them, and rinse out the
milking equipment. I put the cream in the stock tank to cool,
and head wearily to the house.

Hazel calls, "Will you pick up the eggs? I didn't have time
this evening."

I pick up the egg basket and methodically gather about 75
eggs. A couple of broody hens want to set. They will never lay
any more eggs that way, so the sooner I isolate them from a
nest, the sooner they will start again. Like Ma used to do, I put
them into confinement for two or three days to help them
forget about setting. I take the eggs into the basement where it
is cooler and come upstairs again. It is almost eight o'clock

when I remember I am supposed to go to Sunday School teachers' meeting.

I take some cold water down to the basement and wash off the worst of the dirt and sweat. Back upstairs I put on clean clothes and give Hazel an embrace. I drive the old Chevie to the home of a neighbor to study the Sunday School lesson under the tutoring of our pastor. It is an interesting lesson. A cup of coffee, a light lunch, and I'm on my way home.

I walk quietly up the stairs to our bedroom. Hazel is sleeping, but has left the lamp lit for me. I change into my night clothes and lightly kiss Hazel on the forehead.

"Oh Lord, thank you for her. She is beautiful. Thank you for this day. It's been a good day. Amezzz. . ."

13

Farm Homemaker's Day
Summer, 1936

"Jangle, jangle!" The clatter of the alarm clock bell starts my day just as it does Henry's, the one difference being that I can ignore it the first time it goes off. After only a few seconds he hits the silence button and bounds out of bed.

What a night this has been. So hot! For all my turning and squirming, I couldn't find a comfortable position. Why must it be so hot at night for sleeping, then cooler in the morning when I have to get up?

I faintly hear Henry pull on his clothes and reset the alarm for me, but I fall back to sleep before he leaves the room.

"Jangle, jangle, jangle. . ." I wish Henry would turn that alarm off! But it keeps on making its horrendous noise. I open my eyes and I'm alone. I faintly remember how good it had felt to roll over and go back to sleep, but wasn't that only a couple of minutes ago? Knowing that Henry will soon be in for breakfast, I reluctantly rise and face the day.

I dress and retrieve the light blanket from the floor, fold it and the two wrinkled sheets and lay them in the storage compartment in the bottom of our combination sofa-bed. I push the front half of the bed over the back half, then camouflage it with a flowered print couch cover. I top that with a pair of matching pillows, propping them against the wall. Our 16-foot-square bedroom becomes a living room for the day. One corner serves as our dining area with a small table against the wall between two windows that overlook a parched front lawn. Off to one side, a small room that had once been a large closet is now our small kitchen and wash-room. Two other upstairs rooms along with the downstairs are being used by the rest of the family.

Still half asleep, I make my way into the kitchen and pump up the pressure on the old gasoline cookstove. From the pail on a little table next to the stove I dip two cupfuls of water and pour them into a well-worn aluminum kettle I have set on a burner.

Now, how long will it take me to get heat under there, I wonder.

This old stove has some rather unusual tricks about it. Before it will light, I must strike two matches together to get enough flame. While I hold them under the end of a thin tube called the generator, I hope my timing is right when I open the valve to the burner. I'm lucky! A hot blue flame comes to life beneath the kettle. I brush a speck from one of three fresh eggs before slipping them into another small kettle of water. My luck holds as I light the second burner and the water is soon getting warm.

Why did you use that burner? I scold myself. You know the air hasn't been adjusted on it since it started making those yellow tips on the flames. Now you'll have to scour more soot off the bottom of that pan!

When the first water starts boiling, I pour an estimated amount of oatmeal into it, stirring round and round while the eggs diddle in their simmering water. The heat coming up from the burners is a preview of the temperatures I can expect for the rest of the day.

Breakfast is ready none too soon. I hear Henry's heavy work shoes clomping up the stairs. He will be in a hurry to eat because the farm work is piling up. All this heat is not only rushing the growth of the crops, but it makes it hard to keep ahead of the weeds.

I get the smell of cows as Henry comes into the room. I

watch as he gives his face and hands a token washing, then he comes eagerly toward me. Does he expect me to hug something that smells more like a cow barn than the nice country air he is supposed to have been working in?

"Whew! Where have you been!" I ask him.

"Oh, that smell? Hans gave me a shampoo with her tail. That didn't exactly make her my favorite cow!"

"Well, you'd better have a soap shampoo if you're going to get close to me."

He takes the "hint," gets some soap and water and washes most of Hans' "scent" away.

I guess if he can live with it all day, I should be able to tolerate it for a few moments. Besides, I need a little moral support. I am rather emotional these days as we are expecting our first child. That, along with the hot weather and lack of good rest has me feeling tired and somewhat down. However, the thought that I'll soon be holding our own baby in my arms makes it worthwhile.

Breakfast is over in minutes and Henry is out of the door. Before I can wash dishes, I must get water out of the eight-gallon milk can that's down on the porch. Henry's mother and brother Bill, who live downstairs, are having breakfast when I walk through their kitchen.

The pail of water seems heavy, but I get it upstairs and place a kettle of water on the stove. When it is hot, I pour it into my two-gallon dishpan on the kitchen cabinet. Oh, how I wish I had a sink and running water! But we are just starting out and it will take some time before we can afford that luxury. Perhaps, one day, we can even have electricity for lights. What a dreamer! Right now there are too many things to do without spending my time daydreaming.

First of all I must clean all the milking equipment. I wash the cream separator on Mother Schut's large kitchen table. She has already heated water for me and greets me with,

"Good morning. How are you this morning? Could you sleep with all that heat?"

"After a fashion, " I reply. "Toward morning I was able to rest. I guess the baby was hot, too. It kicked me a lot."

"I hope you won't have to carry it too much longer," Mother says sympathetically.

"I do too. But even two months more does seem like a long time."

I dismantle the separator bowl. It is filled with 30 cone-shaped metal discs that are about four inches across. Each one is numbered and slotted and must be put back in the correct order after I wash them. It's a time-consuming task and I really don't feel up to it. Before I'm done, Mother Schut says, "Here, let me finish them."

I'm in no mood to disagree with her, so it's easy to hand over the brush and washcloth. While she finishes the job, I sit and visit with her. Mother Schut is very precious to both Henry and me, especially so to me because my own mother died when I was two and a half years old.

After Mother has stored the clean separator utensils on the enclosed porch, I go out to the garden. Perhaps I can do some weeding before it gets too hot again. The plants look sick and are withering from the intense heat and dry air. There won't be much produce if it doesn't rain fairly soon. I can't really do much with the hoe. The ground is so hard that it takes more power than I can provide.

Returning from the creamery, Henry parks the car by the porch door and runs to the barn, hardly looking my way. I know I must get the butter I had ordered out of that hot car before it becomes soup. Also, the chicken mash must be taken from the sack and carried to the chicken house. After I have taken the butter into the house, I pick up a small pail and fill it with chicken mash. I fill the feeders, then walk to the stock tank for some water to fill the water troughs. By that time, Henry has the horses hooked to the cultivator and is ready to go out to the field. But, since it is nearly 10 a.m., Henry comes in and we go upstairs to the kitchen for coffee and a sandwich. It seems as though he can always eat.

I had noticed that the egg mash came in an exceptionally pretty cotton sack. Whenever he can, Henry buys two or three sacks with the same pattern so I can have enough to sew a dress or apron.

As careful as I had been in pulling the white string and unraveling the stitching at the top of the sack, there were still some threads pulled in the material. I figure I'll be able to work around it, though. I cross the yard shaking the bag inside out and leaving clouds of dust hanging in the still air behind me. I'm feeling sorry for Henry and the horses. They'll have a long day out there in that hot sun. I guess I'm feeling sorry for myself, too. "I wish he had bought more sacks like this one before they are all gone," I say to nobody. "Anyway, this one is nice." I roll the sack into a crumpled ball and carry it rather possessively into the house.

Mother Schut is admiring the print. I will have to soak it in cold water to remove the label. I decide to sew some more clothes for the baby-to-be. I still have to cut old bed sheets to make smaller ones for the crib we'll be borrowing from a friend. Then, too, the diapers I cut from a large piece of flannel will have to be hemmed. It takes a lot of leg power to operate Mother's machine, but it's better than having to sew it all by hand.

After working at it for only a short time I go back upstairs to prepare dinner. The noon meal is our main meal of the day. I peel some potatoes, cook fresh beans from the garden and open a jar of canned pork.

There is barely enough bread left for one meal, so I have no choice but to bake more. The yeast cakes are about a half inch thick, an inch square, hard and dry. I have to soak them in warm water until they dissolve before I can mix them with the flour. The old round bread riser pan that I use for mixing and kneading had long ago been destined for the dump, but was saved because we could not afford a new one.

Working on dinner and kneading the bread has been hard on me, and it is twelve o'clock before I am finished. I know Henry will be in soon for dinner and he doesn't like to wait for his meals. But today he'll have to, at least for a short time.

Hearing the horses and cultivator drive in front of the barn, I hurry to use the 10 or 15 minutes it will take for him to care for the horses. I set the table, check the food on the stove and Henry bounds up the stairs, two at a time, announcing his arrival with, "Wow! That food smells good!"

"Will you bring up a pail of water?" I ask, "And carry out the waste water while I finish the dinner?"

"Sure," he says. "I think I'll get a little fresh water from the pump. That will be colder. It should take only a few minutes."

I can't help smiling. Now I'll have plenty of time to finish making dinner.

In only a few minutes, as he had said, Henry is handing me a dipper of cold, clear water from the pail he has set on the table.

"It's the first cold thing I've tasted or touched all day," I tell him, a spark of life returning to my voice. "Even the milk from the basement was warm."

We sit at our small table and Henry enjoys the hot potatoes, vegetables and meat. My appetite has about disappeared with the heat, but the canned fruit does appeal to me. I have a dish of it with a slice of bread and a glass of milk. In the prayer before and after our meal, we pray for much needed rain, hoping that cooler weather will come with it. Outside, the sun is baking hot and there is not a cloud in the sky.

Henry flops onto the floor; the linoleum rug has a coolness about it. He sleeps for only a short while, then gets up explaining, "I must fix a part on the cultivator while the horses finish their hay. I'll see you at coffee time."

I clear the table and take the meat, milk and butter to the basement where it is some cooler. Those two flights of stairs seem steeper and longer every day. That's just one more reason I look forward to the birth of our baby. How I want to lie down! Even for a short time! But the dishes have to be washed and the bread dough has to be shaped into loaves. As usual, I'll be baking three or four loaves in one long bread pan.

After a brief rest in the straight back chair, I finish those two tasks. Now I can lie down while the bread is rising. I do wish someone would find a way to keep bread longer so I could do more at a time and less often!

I rearrange the pillows on the sofa bed and relax on the flower print cover. It surely is hot in here! Even the little breeze coming in the window is hot!

Then, it's 2 p.m. I must have dozed, but I feel even weaker for it. Won't this heat ever end? I can't feel any worse, so I might as well accomplish something. The floor does need wiping up. Our cheap linoleum rug covers only part of the floor. The rest is just wide painted boards that are hard to get clean and hard to keep that way. But I try.

By 2:30 the bread dough is ready for the oven. I dread the thought of that added heat, but there is no choice. The supply tank needs filling, so I go downstairs to the porch for the two-gallon can of gasoline. This type of stove uses only clear, high-test gas.

Upstairs again, I twist off the pressure cap, pour the fuel through a small funnel into the little opening on the tank, and struggle with the air pump to restore the pressure. Resentfully, I light the oven. I have to watch the gauge until the temperature holds even, because I am the only "automatic" control the oven has. When it is hot enough, I put my four loaves of bread in.

To get away from the heat, I go downstairs. There Mother

Schut is having her daily battle with the hundreds of flies that
find their way from the barnyard into the house. She has hung
up several sticky fly ribbons from the ceiling and is using the
swatter to kill as many as she can, but we are all resigned to
trying to keep their population down just to a point where we
can live with it.

"I'd like to try some of that new-fangled spray that is
supposed to kill every single fly," I tell Mother.

"That I've got to see!" She says and punctuates her remark
with another swat.

Her battle with the flies goes on, but I must get a lunch
ready for Henry. I really don't know what to make.
Everything is so hot. With all this heat coming from the oven,
I wonder if I really need a burner to boil the coffee. But of
course I do, and when the coffee is ready I take it and some
sandwiches outside under a tree. Henry walks out of the
cornfield toward the house. He picks up a small water pail
from the porch and takes it to the pump. He pumps up some
cold water from the well, splashes some on his hands and face
that are covered with sweat and dust, then brings the rest to
me.

"I can't get much done in weather like this," he says. "The
horses are puffing so fast, and they're soaked with sweat. If I
push them any harder they will dry off. Then they'll really be
in trouble. I'll give them a drink of water after lunch when
they've cooled down some."

I'd like to say something to make him feel better, but the
heat is uppermost in my thoughts, too. "I'm baking bread
upstairs," I tell him, "and the way it feels up there, I wouldn't
have had to put it in the oven."

"You do look like you're terribly hot. Here, drink a little of
this cold water."

"I just don't feel like doing anything. I'm so miserable and
I have so much to do."

"The wind is blowing a little and has turned to the

164

northwest. That should help by tonight," he says encouragingly.

"I hope so."

My answer is merely an answer. I don't really put much energy into it. I know I'm not very good company for Henry's lunch break, but at least we are together.

A short time later, Henry leaves for the horses, then for the field. I go upstairs to check the bread. It is about done and rather than walk those stairs down and back up again, I endure the heat until I can take the bread out of the oven. I grease the tops of the loaves and dump them out of the pans onto a folded dish towel that I'll wrap around them later for storing.

Now, what will I get for supper? I wonder. Just enough to keep that husband of mine satisfied. I'll fry some potatoes and warm up the meat left from noon so it doesn't spoil. Henry always likes my fresh bread and jelly, and he can have more sauce if he wants it. Really, I'm not interested in food at all.

I think I'll go outside and put the separator together for the evening milk, give the chickens water and feed. That will save some time for Henry. He'll be pushed for time, because he will be going to a Sunday school teachers' meeting tonight. The sun is a little lower in the sky and the breeze is slightly cooler, as Henry had promised. That will give us some relief.

After finishing those tasks, I walk to the garden and try to pull a few weeds. They won't come out, so I do my best to cut them off with the hoe. Maybe it won't kill them, but they will have to start all over again. When the sweat begins to break out on my face, I feel some better. After several rests and an hour later, I'm almost glad it is time to get supper.

Our room upstairs is still hot and heating more food doesn't help. But the little cross draft between the window by the cot and the two by the table makes it more bearable. Soon I hear the clanging of the cultivator's steel wheels. Through the window I see a couple of hot, tired horses and my husband in the same condition. Some good food and a little rest will put the pep in all their steps.

Our evening meal is always a hurry-up affair. Not much time for talk. But we do take time to pray, read God's word, and even share a short but loving embrace. It sometimes seems as though cows, pigs, and horses are the most important things in life on this farm. But it is our life and our living so I try not to complain even though it's hot.

The dishes must be washed again, but I notice the water pail is nearly empty. The waste pail is full, too, so I decide to wait till Henry can take care of them.

Instead, I go down to the barn to watch Henry milk. I have tried my hand at it, but it seems like my hand muscles just don't work right and I take too long. Henry tells me I spoil the cow by milking that slow, so I let him do it. I'm not overly anxious to milk anyway. Besides, it is easier to visit with him when I am standing near him.

In weather like this the barn is a hot, humid, smelly place. Henry is soon soaked with sweat from being next to the cows' hot bodies. The whole situation is a real heaven for flies. Each cow has brought in a couple hundred of them to add to those already in the barn. The mixture of kerosene and creosote oil that Henry has sprayed lightly on the cows helps a little, but the foot stomping, kicking and tail switching never cease as the cows try to chase away those ever-biting flies.

"I believe I prefer winter to all this," I tell Henry.

"Well, there is one thing to be said for cold weather," he agrees. "There is always a warm spot by the stove, but this heat is everywhere. The radio says a lot of heat records have been broken this summer. And it's not half over!"

"I wonder if we could sleep out on the lawn tonight," I ask him, "With this dry weather there aren't many mosquitoes."

"It's worth a try. Our room upstairs doesn't cool off at all before midnight, but let's wait for some other time. I must go to that meeting tonight."

I watch while Henry milks several cows, but it gets hotter all the time, so I leave for the house. Downstairs at Mother Schut's it is some cooler, as usual.

After an hour or so Henry rushes into the house. He takes a pail of water to the basement, pours it into a washtub and washes off a lot of the dust and sweat. The rest goes on the towel. But he works too hard for me to object. He rushes upstairs to dress in a cool shirt and trousers and is ready in a short time. He kisses me good-bye and is gone.

The wind is blowing a bit, so I take the water pail out and hang it on the pump spout. Then I pull a valve lever so the water will flow into the pail instead of the stock tank. At the rate the windmill is pumping it will take a good half-hour to fill the pail, so I go upstairs to put the cooled bread away. I also finish some work I had left in the afternoon, and it is getting dark by the time I get back to the pump. The water is running over the edge of the pail, but it doesn't matter. That's what keeps the grass so green around the pump.

The cows are reaching deep into the stock tank, so I push the valve lever back again and leave the windmill running. It's a long slow hike, carrying the full pail back to the house. I know the water won't stay cold for long, but it is wet.

It's nine o'clock and getting darker. As I sit by the west window, a slight breeze blows over me. It feels so good.

I light the kerosene lamp and set it near me on the table so I can do some hand sewing. Before long, my spirits are revived. I do wish Henry were home. It's lonesome sitting here alone. It will be an hour or more before he comes home. I think I'll go to bed and catch up on some of the sleep I lost last night. After opening the cot and putting the sheets on it, I change to my cool night clothes and think of how my life revolves around my husband. I turn down the lamp and thank God for my home and Henry and our baby-to-be, and I pray for our health. God is good. I quickly fall asleep.

<u>14</u>

A Winter Day on the Farm
1936-1937

"Jingle, jangle, jingle, Wham!" Silence. That familiar but
unwelcome noise starts another day. It's a quarter past five
and the morning is cold and dark. The bed is so cozy! I
reluctantly pull back the blanket, roll over and half fall out of
bed. I grope around the room for the dresser, then find a
match, strike it on the floor, pull the glass chimney from the
old bedroom kerosene lamp and put the match to its wick. It
flutters a moment, then everything is dark again. I light
another match and notice the kerosene is nearly gone and the
wick is too short to reach it. I shake the lamp to soak the wick
and try again. A feeble yellow flame arises. I give the lamp
another shaking and set the chimney back in place. Finally,
there's enough light to find my clothes.

As the layers of a fleece-lined union suit, heavy socks, wool
flannel shirt, one bib overall, then another one over that, and a
pair of wool shoes with leather soles go on, my teeth gradually
stop chattering. The lamp gets another shake and I stir up the
coals in the wood heater. I put in some kindling and couple of
wood blocks and open the draft below. It really must be cold!
I remember getting up and putting in extra wood around 2
a.m. and it still feels close to freezing in here. I shake the lamp
again. Dumb thing! I'll have to remind Hazel to put in a new

169

wick. Or maybe she can stitch a little strip of underwear on the end of this one and get a couple more weeks use out of it.

I stand a moment by my son's bed. He is sleeping so peacefully. I am a bit envious of my wife. She looks so restful, but she is really tired. The baby has been fussy. I reset the alarm for seven. Breakfast will be ready and welcome by eight, I hope. I blow out the lamp, which is nearly out anyway, and feel my way to the kitchen.

Wow! It is cold! I light the big Rayo lamp on the table which throws a bright glow all around the room. There is a skin of ice on the drinking water by the sink. I lift the lids from the old cookstove, place crumpled paper, kindling and a couple sticks of good maple wood in its firebox. I open the damper to the chimney, then the draft, then light the paper with a match and replace the lids. The flames take off with a roar. I fill the tea kettle from the pail of drinking water and place it on top of the stove. Thin pieces of ice swirl around the top opening as I put on the cover, but they will soon melt and it will all be boiling by the time Hazel gets up.

The kerosene lantern for outdoors hangs on a nail over the basement stairs. Its supply tank on the bottom is full and its glass globe is sparkling clean, thanks to Hazel's busy hands. A quick downward push of the thumb-lift lever pushes the globe assembly up, exposing the wick so I can reach it with a lighted match. The flame flares up with a bright yellow glow and I let the glass down slowly to prevent it from blowing out the flame.

It's time to go to the barn. But first, more layers to ward off the cold. On top of the three or four thicknesses I already have on, I add a heavy knit sweatshirt, a flannel-lined blue denim jacket, a heavy wool cap with fur-lined ear flaps and a pair of four-buckle overshoes. Wool-lined mittens complete the outfit. All this clothing must weigh over 10 pounds and is very restricting. I dip a couple gallons of water out of the five-gallon reservoir fastened to the side of the cookstove. The cast

iron has retained enough heat to keep it warm over night. I
take the bucket of water to the table, pick up the lantern, then
open the door to the porch. The tarpapered screen door has
helped keep out some of the winter's blast, but I must use my
foot to kick away the bank of snow that has drifted against it
on the porch. I'll have to get the door open at least far
enough to squeeze through with the pail and light. The sharp
northwest wind hits me hard as I step out. I must climb
through several more drifts before I reach the barn. About
halfway, the wind blows out the lantern. There is no use trying
to light it there, but I can see well enough to find the barn
door. After stomping through the two-foot drift in front of it,
I open only the top half of the door. Steam from the animals'
breath and bodies billows out through the doorway and warms
my face. Climbing over the bottom of the door, I nearly fall
into the dark barn, then pull the door shut and fumble in my
pockets for a match. I strike it on the metal of the lantern and
quickly light the lantern, then carefully place the still-flaming
match on the damp floor and crush it out with my wet boot. A
fire would be a catastrophe. There is no local fire department,
and it would take nearly a half-hour for the nearest neighbor
to arrive with his team of horses to give any help. Obviously,
fire prevention is a way of life for everybody.

I hang the lantern on a nail protruding from an overhead
wooden joist. Just as in the summer, the horses are waiting for
their breakfast. But now they need about six to eight ears of
corn with their forkful of meadow hay.

By now, most of the cows are standing and some have
dropped manure on their bedding. I clean it off with a fork
and pull clean straw back from the sides of their stalls to give
them nice fresh beds again. It is impossible to keep the
hindquarters of each cow clean, even with the 16-inch gutter
behind them. It is eight inches deep, but that doesn't
guarantee a thing. A quick going over with a curry comb

before each milking is a daily routine and each cow gets a more thorough grooming once or twice every week.

While milking, I go through much the same motions in winter as in summer, except maybe I lean a little tighter against the cows' bodies. Their normal temperature is around 101 degrees Fahrenheit and feels good to me.

I take the milk can from the little "milk house," place it on the concrete alley, and slip the strainer on top of the can. I carry the milk bucket, the pail of water and my one-legged stool to the first cow.

The water to wash her udder with is no longer hot, but there is no more heated in the house so it will have to do. Spot doesn't seem to mind, and I soon have a bucket full of milk. It takes me about an hour and a quarter to finish milking all 10 cows. But the time flies by. As always, it has been a good time to think and plan. The milking, washing, milking becomes an automatic process and leaves my mind free to wander. I go over the plans I had made while milking last summer, discarding some, remaking others, and realizing happily that at least some of the more important ones had been fulfilled. Come springtime, my winter plans would be re-evaluated in light of the existing weather, the prices of farm products, the cost of seed and feed, and other such changes.

Suddenly, it's time to separate the milk. But first, a milk break. I dip the tin cup that always hangs on the wall into the warm milk. I especially relish the feel of the milk on my empty stomach this morning. The pleasure lingers as I place a large pail under one spout and the smaller cream pail under the other. It takes the usual 60 seconds to wind up the separator to full speed. I open the supply tank faucet and skim milk and cream are quickly pouring from the spouts. The separator keeps on spinning as I let go of the drive handle momentarily to refill the supply tank with whole milk or to exchange the full slop pail for an empty one. The cream can seldom needs to be changed, as these 20 gallons of whole milk will produce only about two and a half gallons of cream. That much cream will yield about six pounds of butterfat at the creamery. On our last cream check, the price was 18 cents per pound, so I will receive about one dollar from this morning's batch of milk. However, the skim milk will help the pigs grow and I can expect a few cents back from each can of it by way of a better and bigger hog.

Well, the cows are about ready for their feed, but, as in the summer, I must first clean what's left from last night's corn stover out of their mangers. I use my hands to throw the shredded, woody stalks into the cows' stalls for added bedding. Then I dole out the basketful of grain to the cows according to their milk production.

The heifers we have kept from last summer are reminding me I have forgotten to give them their breakfast. I take a five-gallon slop pail of skim milk to their corner pen and fill two calf pails with a gallon each of skim milk. I hold them in front of the two slots in the fence as all four calves try to force their heads through at the same time. I push two heads back with my foot. "You'll have to wait," I tell them as I struggle to keep the pails upright. Thirty seconds later the pails are empty and the process is repeated with the other two calves being the winners. Next, they should have some whole oats. (Oats are supposed to be better for them than ground grain.) I pour the oats into the dark corner of the calf pen, more or less where the feed bag should be, but only a small part of them hit this mark. The 30-second drink out of the pails hasn't really satisfied the calves' sucking instinct, so they aren't very interested in their oats. They prefer to suck each other's wet ears or lick a favorite spot on the wall.

I pick up two pails full of skim milk that must be carried to the hogs (a simple enough chore in the summer) and walk to the door. But when I try to open it —whoops! I forgot. It is blocked by a snowdrift. I set the pails down, get the scoop from the grain bin and climb over the bottom door. The tracks I had made nearly two hours before have disappeared under a blanket of new snow. It takes several minutes to shovel part of it away so I can swing the door open enough to pass through with the milk. There is no path and it's still quite dark. It's not easy to carry the two pails of milk through the drifts, but it is not very far to the hog house. The hogs have heard me and are squealing from about where the trough should be, but I can see only a dim outline of it in the snow. Why didn't I wait till after breakfast when it would have been lighter! Not wanting to carry the milk back to the barn, I use my booted foot to push the snow aside and clean out the trough as best I can. The hogs push and shove me around and I kick a few of them on their snouts which doesn't stop them at all. Finally, I pour the steaming milk into the trough. The hogs slurp it up and gulp it down. The return trip to the barn is much easier. The pails are empty and I can step in the deep tracks I made coming out. The yellow glow from the lantern that's hanging behind the cows gives barely enough light for me to see the outlines of the mangers. Fortunately, I know where they are. The cows have all eaten their feed and are waiting for alfalfa hay. I carry some to them from a loose stack under the hay chute. Finally! It's 7:30 and time to go see if breakfast is ready. After a night's sleep and two hours of work the appetite has become good, to say the least.

The cream must be carried to the house, left on the back porch for an hour to cool and then added to the large can collected from the last two days. As I lift the lantern from its nail, I notice carbon has darkened the glass globe. I expect that I must have turned the wick up too high. I'm always trying to squeeze more light from the thing, but the result is usually less because the smoke from a high flame collects on the inside of the globe. Oh, for some good light! There have been rumors of electricity coming to the country. That will be the day!

I open the porch door and hear Hazel busy with breakfast

preparations. That's great! I pull off my overshoes and open
the kitchen door. The aroma of fresh side pork fills the air
and oatmeal is bubbling in a kettle on the stove. My jacket
and overalls announce the fact that cows and horses have an
aroma of their own which supersedes any food smell, but it
doesn't bother us too much. Our noses are conditioned to it.

After removing my jacket and cap, I take a small dipper of
hot water from the stove reservoir and pour it into the round
white enamel wash basin. My fingers tingle as I push them
hard against the bottom, and a warmth oozes upward from my
wrists. The bar of strongly-scented soap does wonders for my
hands and face, but the overalls "smell" on. The wash water
should be poured into the waste pail under the sink. Well, I'll
have to empty that before I can dump more in. Wow! There is
even a little ice on the waste water, though the room feels
warm. Hazel has kept the fire going and a couple of the stove
lids are so hot they're turning red, but it takes time to heat up
the whole kitchen.

Winter breakfasts taste better than any other meal partly
because the cold weather whets the appetite and partly because
it is a time I can be alone with Hazel. The baby is still
sleeping. We ask God to bless the good food, then finish off
the bread, pork and oatmeal in a very short time. I take the
Bible and read the chapter about sowing seed in a field. That
seems a long way off for this farmer. A prayer of thanks and
we can sit and talk for a short time. It's great to be alive!

But the reverie can't last. It's daylight and time to get at the
chores again. I crawl back into my barn-scented clothes and
push my way out the door, pulling my collar up against the
wind. It's still cold and blustery, but at least I can see.

I first check the heater in the stock tank. The top has been
kept nearly covered with horse manure, but that hasn't kept
the water from freezing. I open up the door of the tank heater
and note it has no fire in it. I go to the barn to get a bunch of
straw, then to the hog house for some corncobs. I place them

all in the heater and top it off with a couple sticks of wood. I reach in my pocket for a match and strike it on the case of the heater. Pushing the straw aside, I drop the lighted match to the bottom and the straw lights up immediately, sparks shooting out of the long stovepipe like a sparkler on the fourth of July. Wow! This is positively the coldest place on the farm. The wind must come directly from the North Pole.

I check the water level. The tank is only half full. I walk to the pump to put the windmill in gear. But first I must check to see if the pump rod is frozen fast. I slip the pump handle through a slot and stick a bolt through both the handle and the pump rod. Sure enough the rod won't move. It is frozen solid. "Hope Hazel has some boiling water," I mutter, as I walk to the house. Ha! I'm lucky. She hasn't started washing dishes yet.

She offers me the teakettle. "Here," she says. "You may have this, but I hope you won't need all of it. I don't have much water left in the house."

"I'll fill the eight-gallon can when I get the pump thawed out," I promise.

"You didn't empty the waste pail, either," she reminds me.

"I'll do that when I bring you the water."

"Okay," she answers, but I can just see her mind rearranging her morning work pattern.

The pump rod comes loose quite quickly and I check the bolt where I hooked the windmill rod to it. Next I set the windmill in gear. I also put the water can under the pump spout and turn the valve to deliver water to the surface instead of the the underground pipe that carries it to the stock tank. The big blades of the wheel on top swing quickly into the wind. Soon the water is coming from the spout. I fill the nearly empty teakettle and carry it back to the house to trade for the waste-water pail which I take out behind the chicken house and, with the bale handle in one hand and the bottom of the pail in the other, I whoosh it over the dirty frozen mound made from the many pails of waste dumped there before. A fine soapy foam soon forms, then dies, sliding down the mottled ice. At the bottom, the cold liquid cuts deep under the fresh snow and disappears. There, that's done! But the dishwater and baby's bath water will have it full again by noon.

It seems like I spend so much time carrying fresh water into the house and waste water out, sometimes I wish it would run in and out by itself! I return the pail to the house, go back to the pump, carry the can of water to the house and return to the stock tank. I would have minded all that chasing a lot more, only I had caught a few strains of a tune Hazel was humming somewhere off the kitchen while I had been in the house. The tank heater needs more wood. Remembering Hazel's happy voice, I feel warm as I plod my way to the woodpile.

There is nearly an inch of ice over the water in the stock tank. That would take a long time to thaw out, so I get a six-tined fork, break the ice into chunks and lift them out with the fork. I throw the ice to the side of the tank. Now the water will heat faster. The fresh water coming in from the pump will also help it enough for the cattle to drink.

Now, into the barn for the rest of the chores. I harness the horses to pull the manure sled out to the field. Next I open the north door to let the cattle out to drink. The steam billows out and cold air rushes in. Those cows aren't too enthused about going, but it has been nearly 24 hours since their last drink, and they are thirsty. They run out to the stock tank and crowd selfishly against each other to drink. It will take some time before they are all satisfied.

In the meantime, I do the job I dislike most—cleaning the barn. To start with, I roll the manure carrier in on a cable that has one end attached high inside the south end of the barn and the other end to a tall pole out in the cow yard north of the barn. When not in use, it is held up out of the way by a hook above the north door. This carrier looks like a barrel cut in half lengthways. It holds about 25 gallons and has a "trip" that holds it in place while it is being filled, and releases it to flop over to unload it outside. When it is extremely cold, I usually dump the manure by the pole on the far end of the cable, where it remains until spring. Then it will be hauled out to the field and spread on the cropland. Today, even though it is so cold out, I'll dump it onto a flatbed that's on the sled and haul it out to the field. The time I spend on it now will save me more precious time in the spring.

I scrape the manure that missed into the gutters, then scoop it along with the rest up into the carrier. By the time I have emptied it for the third and last time, the cows are anxious to get back in. I hurry to the straw pile in the cow yard and bring back two forkfuls for bedding. More hay goes into the mangers and everything is ready there. When I open the door the cows come rushing in. I fasten each stanchion as the heads poke through, then quickly close the big north door. By now the barn is cold, but the air is much fresher. It won't take long before it is warm again.

I now must hitch the team to the sled and haul the manure to the field. They don't seem any more enthused about it than I am. First I take off my outer jacket and put on a long heavy overcoat that I keep in the barn just for this purpose. I couple up the horses, open the gate and drive them to the sled. A moment later we are out of the cow yard and on our way.

We are a quarter mile into the field before I can tell where I had spread the last load. I stop the team just beyond, in what I figure were the tracks we left before. I throw one forkful of manure at a time, trying to spread the lumpy gook evenly. But it is a cold job and I'm not about to waste time working for perfection. As soon as I am done and turned homeward, the horses break into a snowy trot. I unhook the sled under the carrier cable, ready for tomorrow's load, and in a few minutes the gate is shut, the horses are in the barn, and I have the harnesses hanging against the wall. I feed the puffing pair and give all the horses a rubdown with curry comb and brush. Though time consuming, this job is much more pleasant and satisfying than cleaning up after cows. The chill has already eased, and the horses all but purr in appreciation. Well, one doesn't. She is ticklish in places and she does her best to discourage my grooming efforts.

The hogs have buried themselves under the straw pile in the pole shed. But it shouldn't take much persuading to get them out for breakfast. Maybe I'd never win a hog calling contest, but the couple of "hooey's" I let out bring these critters on the run. The strong north wind across the wide unprotected area between the pole shed and feeder slows them down considerably. They stay out only long enough to bite a few kernels from an ear before deciding this is no fit place to be eating. They each take an ear of corn into their mouth and head back for their warm nest. When that's gone, they brave the cold to get another. A couple of them wise up and carry two at a time. These hogs are all sows, the mothers of the next generation of pigs. When March or April comes, I will have to prepare the hog house for the new families. Each sow now weighs about three hundred pounds and is pregnant. The gestation period (from conception to birth) will be about 110 to 115 days.

I notice their trough is completely embedded in ice. The milk, water and feed left from other days has built up in and around it. I will have to chop some of the frozen mess away so there is enough room for all the hogs to eat at once. Come the next warm day I'll be able to lift the rest of the ice out in large sections. As for now, the dull "chop, chop" of the shovel hitting wood and ice tells me it will be a while yet.

Time now for a coffee break! The kitchen is warm and the coffee is hot. That takes my chill away, both inside and out. Hazel has washed the dishes in a dishpan on the kitchen table, cleared it, and is now busy washing our young son. This must also take place on the kitchen table. He is having a great time grabbing at everything within reach. Hazel dresses him and asks, "Here, do you want to hold him awhile?"

What is sweeter than a little one lying contentedly in your arms? What a precious bundle of joy!

"Will you haul out the ashes from the stoves? And while you have your coat on, you may empty the garbage pail." She really does have a nice way of suggesting these unpleasant jobs. Just as though I had a choice! But, considering that I take care of the "toilet" needs of the cows, horses and pigs, I shouldn't really complain about doing this little chore, too.

I accomplish the task and note the windmill is still pumping water, so I check to see if the stock tank is full. Well, almost, and most of the ice is thawed. I shut off the windmill and decide to spend the last 45 minutes of the morning in the house by the warm stove.

Relaxing, I wonder whether we'll get any mail today. I'm sure an auto won't be able to negotiate all of the roads in our area, but perhaps the mailman will be able to drive through ours since it is one of the most traveled roads in the township. If he does, we will quite likely receive the mail for a dozen of our neighbors that he can't reach.

After an hour of reading farm magazines and newspapers, we sit down to a dinner of home-canned pork with gravy, potatoes, canned beans and some applesauce. Lots of home-made bread, milk and butter add to the menu.

The warmth from the stove, my full stomach and the morning's work in the fresh air make a proper com-bination for a short snooze on the floor near the fire.

But not for long. The woodpile must be split and some wood hauled into the porch for the week ahead. Though the sun is shining, the wind is still blowing the snow around. It takes a half-hour to shovel paths to the barn, chicken house and woodpile.

The chickens need feed, water and fresh straw. That means

climbing through 10 rods (over 150 feet) of drifts to the straw pile, granary and water tank.

There is ice on their drinking trough. That means a trip back to the kitchen stove reservoir for hot water. By this time the eight-gallon can of water in the house is empty, so it's out to the pump for a fill-up. I hope that will last till morning!

Now I can spend a couple of hours splitting wood if my feet don't get too cold. The exercise keeps me warm and soon it's time for a coffee break. What would I do without them?

The sun is nearly down when I saunter out to start the evening chores. It's a repeat performance of feeding horses, pigs, chickens and cows. I throw hay and corn stover down from the haymow before it gets dark so I'll have it handy for both the evening and morning feedings. I coax the fire along again in the tank heater, adding a little kindling and a large chunk of wood to hold overnight.

I get the separator utensils and milk pails from the house and assemble them, ready for the evening's milk. By 5:30 it's dark and I light the old kerosene lantern which makes a feeble attempt to give me light. Six o'clock and it's supper time. That does have an appeal! The hash browns, meat and sauce fortify me for the hour and a half that lies ahead—a carbon copy of the morning's tasks except for the barn cleaning. About eight o'clock I plod back with the yellow finger of lantern light, to Hazel.

It's time for a little relaxation and conversation with the family. Ten o'clock bedtime comes quickly. Before I can crawl in, I must check the animals once more. Old lantern goes along. I throw the corn stover to the cows and some hay to the horses and clean up the stalls behind the cows as they are contented by their cud. They look dreamily at me as though to say, "Thank you. We are feeling great. You just go to bed."

The quick cold trip brings me back to a warm home, a

loving wife and a wonderful son. The day has been long, the weather cold, but I am grateful for what the day has brought.

Several chunks of wood in the stove and several more behind it, and we crawl between the soft flannel sheets and thank God for his blessings and ask that he watch over our tomorrows.

15

How We Raised Corn

If Grandpa Schut could only walk in our cornfields today! His memories of horses and hard work would be a stark contrast with the tractors and machinery he'd see.

He'd remember stories of how the first settlers that came to Minnesota had planted their corn in starter plots (small areas where they had prepared the soil very carefully). That was, maybe, before the 1860s. When their regular fields were ready and the corn was well sprouted, the farmer transplanted each young plant by hand.

Besides breaking the ground into a very fine texture, they would have wanted to do everything else possible to insure the best germination and the liveliest sprouts they could produce. I imagine several things were considered in choosing the location for a starter plot: richness of soil, availability of moisture, and perhaps even the distance from the farmhouse and field.

It seems to me that moving those tender little corn plants would have stunted their growth and even cause a number of them to die. However, because their corn took longer to mature than our hybrids, plus the fact that it took them many times longer to prepare a whole field for planting, those early Minnesota settlers may have felt that a small loss was more than compensated for by the head start it afforded the crop in this area's comparatively short growing season.

The old story we all hear about the Indians having taught

the New Englanders to bury a fish under each hill of corn did make sense. The added fertilizer was a good idea. However, I never knew of anyone in our area who had done that.

Both Grandpa Schut and I would remember the old hand planter we kept around the farm just to replant places where nothing came up. Perhaps a few seeds had been bad, the seeder had skipped, or the pesky chipmunks, gophers or squirrels had dug them up for dinner.

I can just hear what Grandpa would say, standing next to my Massey Harris tractor. "Oh, so much noise! So much stink!" While he would admire its power and ability, he'd regret, as I do, the loss of intimacy with the soil and cooperation between man and horse. That might seem a hard price for him to pay, even for today's bountiful harvests. The smell of horse sweat along with our own made a "perfume" you might call "essence-of-accomplishment." Though it was not desirable among company, it was honorable in the fields.

I'm sure Grandpa and his contemporaries often dreamed of having a far better way to work their land, just as the women dreamed of having an easier washday and clothes that didn't need ironing. Although they might not have expected it, the dream was there.

But a person works with what he has, so most of the pioneers plowed with horses or oxen. (For those who don't know, oxen are bulls that have been castrated, making them easier to handle.)

It was important to have the corn grow about 42 inches apart in rows that same distance apart. This "checking" allowed room for cultivating across the rows as well as along them. To make the spacing accurate, a marker sled was drawn back and forth across the field, tracing lines into the loose soil. Drawing it crosswise marked off squares, thus the "checking." The small hand planter was used to plant the corn wherever lines met. These places were call "hills."

That old hand corn planter was a simple but ingenious device. Its main parts were a pair of wooden boards, each about a yard long, three inches wide and an inch thick. A three-inch-square piece of sheet metal formed like a shallow scoop was fastened to the bottom end of each board. A metal pin fastened the two pieces of metal together and served as a hinge for the two uprights. A round handle was bolted onto each board a couple of inches from their tops and sticking outward at right angles from them.

A metal container big enough to hold about two quarts of seed corn was attached to the outside of one of the boards. It had a slot in its bottom where a metal bar ran through and was fastened to the other board. Depending on how the adjustable chamber in the bar had been set, two to five kernels could be dropped at once. When the tops of the uprights were pulled about a foot apart, the metal scoops at the bottom would draw together and catch the seeds as they tumbled down the inside of a long tin tube. While it was in that position, the planter was thrust downward so the metal end penetrated the earth. When the top ends were pushed together again, the scoops parted about three-fourths of an inch, releasing the seeds and planting them one or two inches deep. The farmer would then lift the planter, step lightly on the spot to firm the soil around the seeds and move on to the next hill. He'd repeat the process again and again and . . .

With some practice, a good operator could plant 50 or even 60 hills per minute.

Later on, Pa and I used a two-row planter. It was a complicated machine that required skill and experience to operate. I purchased a tractor planter much later. In fact, not till the 1960s.

At this time, it was still customary to "check" the corn. All rows, no matter which way they went, had to be that same 42 inches apart to accommodate the cultivator. This was accomplished by stretching a heavy wire across the entire length of the field in the direction you were planting. Stakes held the ends securely in place. This wire, with large knots every 42 inches along it, was inserted between several steel pulleys and a movable slotted fork. As the planter was drawn forward by the horses, the knots in the wire would pull the fork back, triggering several gadgets. They planted three or four kernels of corn in each row exactly in line with the knot in the wire. The secret of getting straight rows crosswise was to keep the wire equally tight each time a stake was moved. Pulling the wire three or four inches tighter would pull every knot three or four inches out of line with the kernels of corn that had been dropped in the previous rows. It would then be very difficult to cultivate crosswise. On level fields the task of planting was not bad, but on steep side hills the rows were seldom straight.

Commercial fertilizer became popular in the 1950s. Some farmers used it sooner, but then mostly at planting time as a starter.

Herbicides did not come into wide use until the 60s. When we started using them to control the weeds, checking became no longer necessary. We could then plant our corn closer together in the rows, so the long wire with all its knots was abandoned. Spacing the seeds was now merely a matter of adjusting the planter for the distance apart the corn should be dropped. We still kept the rows an even 42 inches apart, but this was no longer difficult. We merely followed a groove made by a marker on our previous trip across the field. The marker was simply a rod that extended out from the side of the planter far enough so that it would trace a groove into the freshly worked soil exactly where the middle of the planter had to travel for the next two rows.

Cultivating the cornfields usually started when the plants were one to two inches tall. Horses were used to pulling a one-row cultivator. There were several different kinds. Some of the older ones were designed to be pulled by one horse and cultivated the space between the rows. They had no wheels and were merely four to six hoe-like shovels on a frame, with two handles bolted onto the frame. Later, the two-horse, one-row walking cultivator was used. It straddled the row. A steel framework equipped with four or six shovels was mounted on two wheels. A pole between the two horses completed the machine. There was no provision for a seat for the operator. It was called a walking cultivator, but the operator did the walking, and many miles a day.

Later on, riding cultivators came out with a device where we could steer the wheels with our feet while sitting on a seat. That led the way to the building of a two-row cultivator that could be pulled by three or four horses.

Cultivating corn for the first time each year was a slow and tedious job. The horses had to be trained to walk very slowly, around one or two miles per hour. Shields were used between the shovels and the corn plants to prevent the soil from covering up the small plants. These shields had to be positioned just the right height to permit a small amount of soil to roll on the row to smother the little weeds but not cover up the corn.

The second cultivation was usually begun when the corn plants were about three to five inches tall if the weather were favorable, usually a week or ten days after the first cultivation had been completed. When checking was still being done, this cultivation was done crossways, or at right angles to the row. The shields were raised or removed to allow more soil to roll onto the weeds. About one week after that was completed, the third cultivating began. The direction was now the same as that in which the corn had been planted. The horses were urged to move more rapidly and if the shields were still on, they were adjusted to throw more soil toward the row and hopefully cover up all the weeds that had survived the first two cultivations, but without covering up the corn plants. They were usually 15 to 20 inches tall by that time. It took quite a

bit of patience, experience and know-how to adjust the cultivator so as to destroy all the weeds. Sometimes it became
necessary to cultivate the field still another time when the corn
was 20 to 30 inches tall. We usually called this the "hilling"
cultivation because we would adjust the shovels so that the soil
would be thrown in a long mound around the base of the
corn. This was mostly to kill weeds, but also to support the
cornstalks in the hills. It usually took place around the fourth
of July. As the weather was usually hot and humid, the work
was hard for both man and horse. Many horses died of heat
exhaustion when they were not given enough water and rest.

During this time of intense cultivation, it often became
necessary to use the old hand hoe to destroy the weeds that
escaped. Canadian thistles, milkweeds and sow thistles all had
roots that were crooked and tough. Lots of elbow grease was
needed to cut them off. After the last cultivating, we let the
corn grow until harvest.

Until 1925 very few farms had silos. Even then it took many
years before they became a part of every farming operation.
The first time I helped to fill silo was about 1924. Our
neighbor had a large wooden stave silo.

One big problem was the lack of suitable power to operate
the silo filler, a cutting and blowing machine. That first time I
helped with the silo filling, it was powered by a 12-
horsepower, one-cylinder engine with huge flywheels five feet
in diameter. The corn was cut and tied into bundles by a
binder that was pulled by three horses. The bundles were
placed on a "rack and wagon" that was pulled by two horses.
This task was a muscle builder and a back breaker. If the corn
were tall and green, some bundles would weigh as much as 70
pounds. It was almost impossible to lift them with a fork.
Many times it became necessary to lift them by hand or have
another man help put the bundle on the wagon.

After piling the bundles as high as we could, the load was
taken to the silo filler and unloaded one bundle at a time onto

a conveyer belt. This moved it to the rotating knives which would cut it into half-inch bits and blow it up the pipe to the top of the silo and into a series of short distributor pipes.

It was thought at the time that the silage had to be distributed evenly within the entire circumference of the silo and then be tamped down by as many feet as possible. In that first silo I helped with, there were five boys my age. We would have to tramp around and around on the fresh silage as it came from the distributing pipe. We would take turns holding the pipe, as that was considered a privilege. Every three feet, as the silo filled, we would take off a length of pipe and pass it down the chute to the ground. The silo was 14 feet in diameter and 30 feet high. It took a week to fill it. Gerrit Dykhuizen, Jake and Herman Balster, my brother Bert and I spent most of the week tramping around in there. We had a good time and earned a little money doing it.

Within a few years our neighbors bought a new 10-20 McDeering tractor. It was then used to furnish power for the silo filler. We were able to cut the filling time by over 50 percent. As the years went by, nearly every farm had its silo and it was discovered that the silage did not have to be tamped and distributed until the silo was nearly full.

The field choppers and self-unloading wagons began to appear in the 1950s. That eliminated the hardest work on the farm and with it one of the last farm tasks taking six to eight farmers working together. Now two or three workers could fill a silo in one day.

Those times were the beginning of a trend away from farming methods in which every farmer was dependent on his neighbor to get many of his farm tasks done. Combines replaced the threshing crews, the field corn picker replaced the husker and shredder with its crew, and the field chopper needs only two or three men in its crew. The milk truck hauls the whole milk. Formerly only the cream was taken to the creamery, and the neighbors took turns doing that. The chain saw has eliminated the need for a five-man crew to operate a buzz saw. In almost every area of farming the operator can be independent of his neighbor. I can't help but consider the end of that era of interdependence to be regrettable. The memories I hold of working with and caring for each neighbor are the most pleasant I have. Our society has lost one of the greatest reasons for being. Independence is no substitute for a loving, helping, caring relationship among neighbors!

The harvesting of the corn before the mechanical corn binder was a laborious, time-consuming task. A wooden "horse" was made of a pole about 10 feet long with two one-by-six boards about three feet long nailed to it at right angles on one end. These boards were open from each other at about 45 degrees, supported by several thin, light boards to the pole and to each other. The one-by-six boards served as legs.

Cornstalks taken from an area covered by 64 hills of corn were cut with a 12-inch corn knife fastened to a two-foot wooden handle, then placed against this "horse." The corn from half those hills was placed on one side and from the remaining 32 hills, on the other. A stout twine string was then tied about 18 inches from the top. The horse was then pulled from under this "shock" of cornstalks and placed forward for the next shock.

As soon as the corn ears were dry, they were husked and thrown on a pile where the shock had stood and the stalks were tied in large bundles. These bundles were placed in large shocks until they could be hauled to the farmyard to be stacked and used for feed for the cows and horses. The corn ears were picked up into a basket and dumped into a wagon box which held about 50 bushel baskets of ear corn. The ear corn was hauled to a corn crib and stored in it to dry. Some-time during this period, the nicest and largest corn ears were selected and stored in the house to be shelled and used for the next year's seed. Many homes had a small screened room for the seed corn to keep out the ever-present mice. During the winter, this corn was shelled by hand or by a small hand-powered sheller. The shelled corn was stored in metal cans until planting time. A few kernels were selected at random and placed in a testing box of soil to determine its germination strength. The test results determined how many seeds to plant in a hill.

In my youth, there were only a few farmers that still used the hand-cutting method of harvesting corn. The widely used corn binder could cut and bind the standing corn into bundles and deliver it into rows. We would then use the wooden horse to support several bundles until they could be tied up as a shock and stand alone. After two or three weeks, the corn could be husked in the same manner as the hand-cut corn, or could be hauled as bundles and stacked. A machine called a shredder-husker was powered by a large one-cylinder engine or a tractor. It was often used to husk the corn and deliver it into a wagon box. The stalks, husks and leaves were then either shredded into four-to-eight inch pieces and blown into the haymow for cow feed, or blown onto a pile outside, also to be used for feed. The bundles were taken from a stack, or several neighbors would join each other with wagons and racks to haul the corn bundles directly from the shocks to the shredder.

In the 1940s and 50s the county farm extension offices began an intensive campaign to encourage farmers to produce more alfalfa. Corn fodder (or stover, as it was sometimes called) was shown to be very low in feed nutrients, especially proteins. Alfalfa hay was high in protein and added nitrogen to the soil as it grew. Another factor that encouraged the change to alfalfa was that it prevented much of the soil erosion.

This change from corn to alfalfa made the corn fodder nearly worthless as cow feed, so it became the practice of farmers to husk the standing corn directly from the field. A team of horses, a wagon and wagon box with one side built about three feet higher than the other became standard equipment for the corn farmer. For nearly a month or six weeks during October and November, the steady bang, bang of the corn against the bang boards could be heard across the land. It was another back-breaking, muscle-building job. A good picker could pick up to a hundred bushels or two hundred baskets per 11-hour day. That included shoveling the corn off the wagon into the crib both at noon and after dark at night.

Mechanical corn pickers did not come into use in our area as soon as in Iowa or the Dakotas, but by the 1960s most of the corn was mechanically picked and not long after that the picker-sheller combines began to make their appearance.

So, in the period from 1915 to 1980, corn production evolved from almost a completely hand-grown crop to the fertilizer, herbicide, insecticide machine that does the planting and cultivating and the large six-row picker-sheller combine that does the harvesting. One man can now harvest more corn in one hour than I did in a whole week. The key ingredient in that entire change was OIL. If we ever run out of it we could be back to elbow grease and muscle power. Change will have gone the full cycle.

<u>16</u>

Progress on the Farm
1915-1952

In this chapter it is my purpose to record many of the
changes that occurred on farms and in homes between the
years 1915 and 1952. I intend to tell about them in a
chronological sequence as I lived through them on our farm.
The order and dates may differ from other farms, but not by
much. They would have been affected by the type of farming
a person was engaged in. For example a dairy farmer would
have made a milking machine a priority, while a crop farmer
would rather have bought a combine.

There were two prerequisites to change on the farm. First,
the new machine must save time for the farmer. Second, it
ought to eliminate some hard work. This last factor did not
always happen. For example, hauling, carrying, and stacking
hay bales was heavier work than pitching loose hay as we had
done before, but the time saved outweighed that disadvantage.

Most of the change from hand labor (such as hand planting,
hoeing, and harvesting of corn) to mostly horse-drawn
equipment took place before my time. The change from
walking plows and cultivators to riding equipment occurred
during my early lifetime.

Any changes were actually resisted by the older generation.
For one thing, no amount of proof could convince them that a
riding cultivator could do as good a job as a walker, nor could
they be persuaded that a milking machine could milk as well
as a man with his two hands. But no amount of disapproval

could stem the tide of mechanization. The time and hard work that machines could save eventually converted even the most hard-core old timer.

Two factors most responsible for the change in our farm and home were the coming of electricity and the farm tractor.

Electricity in the home made it possible to have automatic control for water pressure, thus, indoor bathrooms. Then came the furnaces, refrigerators, freezers, hot water, fans, washers, dryers and a host of other conveniences that we take for granted today.

On the farm, electricity soon pumped the water for cattle, milked the cows, ran automatic fountains, automatic fans, automatic heat lamps, milk coolers, motors to operate drills, saws, and dozens of other implements. In some instances it just made things easier and more pleasant, but many gadgets simply could not be used without electricity.

Tractors made it possible to perform nearly all farm work easier and more quickly, but the change from horses to tractor machinery went slowly since the cost of buying all new machinery was high. Most farmers kept some horses and used their horse machinery while they replaced it with tractor machinery over a period of years.

Others adapted some of the horse machinery for tractor use until new could be bought. The coming of "power take-off" power to moving machinery caused a dramatic change in handling crops. Some of the first balers and combines had used separate motors, but the cost of maintenance of those extra motors soon caused farmers to use power take-off machinery. The field choppers with self-unloading wagons were the ultimate in saving the hard work of lifting heavy green crops onto the racks and then feeding them into a stationary silage chopper.

The first attempt in our area to harness an engine to do field work was the connection of a huge one-cylinder, 12-horsepower engine to a couple of large steel wheels, intended to be hooked onto a plow. The three Mol brothers, Henry, Jake and Bill, labored months to make the contraption work. This was about 1915-1920.

Around 1928, our neighbor, Henry Dykhuizen, bought a 10-20 McDeering tractor. It had four-inch spade lugs bolted onto its steel wheels, which were about four feet in diameter. These provided good traction, but nearly shook the hat off your head when driving on hard ground. The tractor was a good source of stationary power. It worked well with silo fillers, feed grinders, and the like.

The motor had a hand crank to start it and special trigger to retard the spark until the motor had started. Woe to anyone who forgot to retard the spark! Many arms were broken because of the kickback of the motor.

To us it was a marvel. It pulled two plows and never got tired! And at nearly twice the speed of horses!

Bert and I started to operate Mother's farm in 1925. I was 15, Bert was 13. We had three horses and all horse machinery. We milked seven to ten cows, raised about 30 hogs per year and two hundred hens who laid eggs in the summer but went on strike during the winter.

There wasn't much change until 1938 because the depression and drought were so acute that farmers had all they could do to get enough to eat and pay their interest and taxes. Many of them lost their farms.

From the year of Hazel's and my marriage in 1935, the prices of farm products began to increase. Then the build-up of military supplies and food supplies before World War II caused the economy to grow rapidly. Food prices rose so fast that the federal government imposed price controls during the war.

The war effort caused a shortage of farm machinery and a permit from the county war organization had to be obtained to purchase any machinery. A farmer had to produce evidence that he needed the machine to increase or maintain farm production.

We were fortunate. Through a series of events, we had been able to get a tractor before the United States entered the war.

Ever since our marriage, Hazel and I had dreamed of a honeymoon we never had. In 1941, we decided it would be now or not for years to come. We bought a nearly new 1940 Chevrolet four-door sedan for $650 and in August of that year, with our sons Lawrence and Wayne as our chaperones, we set out for California to visit brother Bert and his wife, Winifred. We took in many of the sights along the way (the Black Hills, Yellowstone Park, Salt Lake City) and finally arrived in Downey, California, near Los Angeles.

We then saw many of the sights in California. (Knotts Berry Farm was only a small restaurant by the side of the road.) Sister Elsie was working in California and she decided to ride home with us. We stopped at cabins over night or, at times, slept in the car. We returned home after three weeks of a rather unusual honeymoon, but we had enjoyed it.

After being home a month, we traded the 1941 Chevrolet in on a new Massey Harris tractor, plow and disk. We received our full $650 in trade for the car and paid about $500 more for the tractor and equipment. We bought a 1936 Chevrolet that we used during the entire war period. We didn't put many miles on it since we were rationed only three gallons of gas per week. Farmers could receive additional rations by certifying their need of it. Because they were allowed all they needed for their tractors, a number of them abused the rationing system and many tractor gas gallons ended up in the gas tanks of cars.

The tractor, plow and disk helped to do the heavy work on the farm which had taken much time to do with the horses, but all the haying was still done with horse machinery. Also, much of the harvesting involved hand labor and horse equipment.

We started our farming career in 1935 by renting everything

from my mother on a 50-50 basis. In 1939 we bought the personal property from Mother and rented the farm from her for cash. The cost of horses and machinery was $640; the cows, $50 to $70 each.

Some interesting facts I found in our records for 1939 showed our total gross income from cream sold was $546.95; hogs sold, $631.81; cattle sold, $198.04; eggs sold, $105.55 and poultry sold, $79.31. Total gross, $1561.66. Expenses were $382.69, not including rent or interest.

Electricity came to some areas in the community between 1935 and 1938, but we didn't get it until 1946. Back in 1939 we had been able to buy a Delco 32-volt generating plant for $45. This included 16 two-volt batteries. After installing it in our basement and wiring our house and barn, we had both lights and radio. About 1944, we ran two heavy special-duty electric wires from our 32-volt generating plant to the barn and bought a milking machine. As the vacuum pumps needed a half-horse power motor, the electric demand of the motor and lights was too heavy for the batteries to supply and the Delco motor had to be started every time we milked. We also put a motor on the cream separator. These conveniences were very helpful, but pumping water was left up to the windmill.

We had wanted desperately to have the water running into the house and to install drinking cups for the cows, but our electric system could not furnish the power to pump water up to pressure. In 1941 we bought a large used creamery churn. This we hoisted up into the haymow of the barn and built an insulated form around it. We had an opening into the barn below so the heat from the cattle could keep the water system from freezing. The windmill could then pump the water from the well through a pipe under the ground and up into the old churn which held several hundred gallons. We then installed a drinking cup for every two cows. This not only saved time but increased milk production since the cows could drink at will.

Because the churn was enclosed, we knew the water was

clean and pure. So we dug down a pipe to the house and had one faucet over the sink. Whoopee! No more carrying water to the house! The tank in the barn was only a few feet higher than the faucet in the house, so we had very little pressure. But it was a tremendous improvement over carrying it. We also had a hand "cistern pump" which pumped water out of a cistern near the house. The cistern was supplied by rain water from the roof. During the summer we usually had enough for washing, but during winter the supply would run out. There was no filter in the system so this water was not fit for drinking or cooking, but because it was soft, it was very desirable for washing and was usually reserved for that purpose.

The supply tank (old churn up in the barn) was filled by the windmill pump when there was wind. There was no way to know how much water was in the enclosed tank, so we installed an overflow near the top to divert any extra amount pumped in. Later I installed a float in the tank which I connected over a series of pulleys to a weight on the outside of the barn. When the weight was up, we knew the float was down and the tank nearly empty. The system worked quite well.

We also discovered that when water ran into the house without any effort much more of it was used and the waste-water pail was always running over. The task of hauling it out became a real problem. So we installed a small septic tank and a drain for the waste water. This proved to be an even greater help than running water into the house. Now we had water coming in and going out by itself! But hot running water, a bathtub and the flushing toilet would have to wait for more electricity.

Electricity came to Silver Creek before it did to us and it brought about a number of changes. Many of the machines that had been powered by steam engine were converted to electric motors. A locker plant was built in 1940 providing a method for keeping meat frozen and eliminating the task of canning and curing our meat at home. All we had to do was remember to take some of it home when be brought the cream to the creamery. It was still a problem to preserve meat after we had it home since we didn't have an electric refrigerator. We did buy an icebox, however, and had ice delivered twice a week. Even this was a great improvement over using cold water from the well or carrying the perishable foods down to the basement.

Remember Pearl Harbor?—December 7, 1941—When the United States entered the war our whole life was affected. We soon discovered we had lost much of our freedom. We were told how much meat, sugar, butter, gas, and even how many shoes we could buy. We could produce our own meat and butter, but sugar was difficult for us. It was carefully rationed to each person. In our home we had small children who received equal sugar rations with the adults, but did not use as much, so we really had enough for our needs. Imagine the consternation of one of our neighbors who had placed sugar in a sack resembling a salt sack. At the time, it was a common practice to sprinkle salt on the loose hay as it was stored in the barn. This neighbor sprinkled his whole sack of sugar on the hay in the barn. Fortunately, the director of rationing in Buffalo was an understanding person and issued new ration stamps to him.

The increase in farm prices placed our income into the price bracket where we were forced to file income tax returns in 1941. However, we paid no tax until 1943 when we sent in $59.99.

Brother Bill worked for us after school and during the summer when I needed him. He also worked for us in 1942 after he graduated.

We rented the farm on which we now live from the Charles Klemz estate. The rent was $180 for 80 acres. The buildings were vacant and of very little use. Later, Clarence Addicks bought the place. He fixed up the house and built a basement barn and a silo.

It may be of interest what kind of cars we owned. Before Hazel and I were married, Mother owned a 1927 Chevrolet. She couldn't drive it, so it was driven by one of us sons. In 1936 we bought a 1928 Model T Ford two-door sedan; in 1938 we traded that in on a 1928 four-door Dodge sedan. It had been owned by Arnold Vandergon and was a good car. Then in 1941 we owned a 1940 Chev for three months (the car that we drove to California on our belated honeymoon), then traded that for a tractor and bought a 1936 Chev. We kept that Chev until 1950 when we bought a nearly new 1949 Hudson, a very good car. We drove it 102,000 miles and in 1960 bought another Hudson which was a lemon. We kept that for only a couple of years when we bought a new 1963 Ford.

Even though the war was causing many shortages, equipment to help the farmer produce more was available after waiting for months. We often bought used equipment, but the demand for it increased its price considerably, often to more than the cost of new. The price of new equipment was controlled by law, but not that of used machinery. A tactic used by implement dealers was to take a new tractor or machine and use it for a day or more and then sell it as a used machine. The price would then be hundreds of dollars more than new.

In 1943, Sam Dykhuizen and I were able to buy a new power take-off Minnesota grain binder to replace the 30-year-old horse-drawn binder we had been using. I also bought a used silo filler at the Dykhuizen auction. In 1944, our neighbors and I bought a used Allis Chalmers thresher and by working together we were able to thresh our own grain. Ervin Klemz, Evert Hofman, Gerrit Dykhuizen, Al Dykhuizen, Sam Dykhuizen and I each owned one-sixth interest in the machine. We also threshed for Ernest Repke. We charged him a fee per bushel.

In 1944, brother Bill and I covered the house where we lived with "Bricksulite" insulated siding. In 1945, Hazel and I bought the 80-acre farm from Mother for $6500. The buildings were old then, and according to our records we had replaced all except the house by 1953.

During the war years, everybody was almost forced to buy war bonds from the government. The most popular type was called Type E. We could buy a $100 bond for $75 which matured in 10 years. The interest rate came to a little more than three percent if you kept them to maturity. There was a penalty for cashing them early.

In 1945 we built our first silo. It was 12 feet in diameter and 20 feet high. We had poured a concrete foundation back in 1937 that was 10 feet deep. In place of the silo we had been using lath corn cribbing lined with a tough paper. The spoilage was high and the cribs had to be put up as we filled them and taken down as we fed from them. We bought 10 feet one year and added 15 feet a year or so later.

Up until 1941 skim milk was largely a by-product in the production of butter and was fed to hogs. The cream was taken to the creamery for churning. War caused a sharp increase in the use of skim milk as food and the price became so high that it was uneconomical to feed it to hogs. In 1943, many other creameries were installing equipment to handle milk and our Silver Creek creamery was losing customers. So a meeting was held and it was decided to put milk handling equipment in there, too. There was strong opposition, as many felt that the high price of milk was only a war phenomenon and would go down after the war, leaving the equipment unused. However, the milk handling equipment did get installed and in 1943 we started selling whole milk instead of just the cream. We received $.85 per cwt. (one hundred pounds) for the skim milk and $.58 per lb. for the butter fat. Our records show that we sold 10,586 lbs. of whole milk in our highest month.

Many farmers continued to keep their skim milk for hogs

and calves, while others sold milk during only part of the year. A few of them never sold milk until there were so few cream farmers that the creamery refused to accept just their cream. At this same time, the milk hauler entered into the picture and we farmers were relieved from the task of hauling either the milk or the cream to the creamery. Collections were made only three times a week for the cream, but the milk had to get to the creamery daily to preserve its freshness.

Two dramatic events took place in 1946. We were hooked up to "central power" electricity and the federal price controls were lifted.

Those controls had been difficult to enforce and much of the produce had found its way into the "black market" at a higher price than the food processor was allowed to pay. Whole milk prices had stayed around $2.50 to $3 per cwt. until August 1946 when the controls were lifted, then they shot up to $4.50 by December of that year. Live hog prices zoomed up over $7 per cwt. This put more money into the pockets of farmers. With the war over, machinery and other products were becoming more available. It was definitely a seller's market and many prices sky-rocketed.

On September 4, 1946, electricity from our local electric "coop" finally came to our farm. We were able to put it to work milking cows, pumping water, and running a radio and toaster all at the same time! We also bought a bathtub and a flush toilet! We kept our icebox until September 1948 when we bought a new refrigerator for $278. There has been a constant stream of electrical appliances coming into our home ever since. Our first electric bill was $4.45.

As our mechanization process continued, we were able to operate more land. We rented some from Mr. Fred Buck near Silver Creek, and some from Isaac Hoglund (later owned by Wm. Cain).

In 1946, the farm on which we now (in 1981) live came up for sale. We bought it from Clarence Addicks for $6200.

There was an old house, a basement barn and a silo on the place. We took possession in 1947 and rented out the house to different people until brother Bill and his wife rented the farm from us for a couple of years (1949-1951).

After the war, many new techniques and products were used. Commercial fertilizer on crops was a new thing for our community. In 1946 we were among the first farmers to use it. The results were so dramatic that in a short time it was a common practice in the area. Artificial insemination of cows began in 1947 and we were one of the first farmers to use it, too. It took several years and some change of methods before that became a common practice.

In 1947, we built the two-car garage on our farm. The floor was poured the next year. I was laid up most of 1948 with a very sore back. Egbert Kuiper worked for us that summer. He stayed by his parents, across the road, at night but ate meals in our home. After going to many doctors, I was able to do my work again in the fall of that same year.

The real estate tax on both farms in 1948 was $187.50.

In 1949, we bought an oil burning space heater for our living room. It heated most of the house. The upstairs rooms were warmed through a register in the floor directly above the stove. At that time, fuel oil was 14.6 cents per gallon. Today it is 96.4 and rising.

Also in 1949 we dug a new sewer east of the present barn and laid it deep enough so we could have a drain in the basement and the washing could be done down there. That same year we put a new roof on the west part of the house.

Our cow herd was increasing, so we needed more room. It was still 1949 when we started a new barn by building a 22- x 34-foot flat-top just northeast of the old barn. We were able to house seven head of young stock, two horses and some calves in this structure. In the old barn, an inside milk house was made from a horse stall and we made room for 15 cows plus a pen for more calves.

In 1950, our neighbors and I (the same group that bought the used Allis Chalmers thresher back in 1944) bought a new McDeering thresher. We also bought a new Model 30 Massey Harris tractor for $215.

We sold our last two horses in 1951, thus committing ourselves totally to tractor farming, something I had not thought possible when we bought our first tractor in 1941. We also bought a new mechanical picker with our neighbor, Gerrit Dykhuizen. Total cost, $950. For $300 we bought a 1941 Chev pickup for farm use and as a second car for our maturing sons.

Mother and Elsie had been living in Holland, Michigan, for several years, but returned permanently in 1951 and built a new home in Silver Creek, just east of the town hall. As Mother needed the money we owed her for the farm, we borrowed $3,500 from the Federal Land Bank at four percent interest and paid her in full.

In 1952, we completed the new barn, making it 64 by 34 feet with a steel round roof. We were able to house 18 cows, along with young stock and calves. Later, we changed the calf pens and added four more cow stalls. The total cost of the barn, including the part built in 1949, was $5200. We then converted the old barn into a hog house and were able to raise 150 hogs per year. Top hog price in 1952 was $19 per cwt; for milk, $4 per cwt (for 3.5 percent butter fat).

In 1952, Gerrit Dykhuizen and I bought a Mulkey elevator for elevating grain and hay into the storage facilities.

That year, too, we quit the chicken business as it was too small to operate efficiently. Besides, our sons had not inherited their grandmother's liking to work with chickens. We moved the henhouse, converted it into a tractor shed and built a milk house on the old site next the new barn.

Part III

Forty-Five Years of
Our Marital Pilgrimage

1

Our Family Grows

Hazel and I were—are—and ever will be different in many ways besides one of us being a woman and the other a man. This has not been all bad. In fact, it has proved to be good.

I am by nature confident, impatient, somewhat domineering and aggressive in both a negative and positive way. I am gregarious, sociable and, I suppose, may be considered by some to be obnoxious at times. I tend not to be precise in my work, but move and work rapidly. Also, I have wide interests.

Hazel lacks confidence in herself, but is meticulous in her work. She is quite reserved, never offends anyone, is sociable to those she knows well, and has limited interests. She has always worked hard and what she does, she does very well. She is an excellent cook and gardener, she sews well and is a top-notch mother and homemaker. We both have strong Christian convictions, deep love for family, and strong family ties. Also, we both come from a Holland background.

It isn't easy to analyze why we were attracted to each other. There was that certain something that she had, and still has, that made her desirable to me as a wife and mother of our children—a role she has carried out with every part of her being, and has done so well. I have never once entertained the thought of wanting someone else to replace her and I believe that feeling to be mutual.

With that as a basis, it was not by accident that our marriage

207

has been a happy one. This does not mean that we had no sorrows, depression, disagreements or difficult times.

To be a farmer and a farmer's wife had not been our first choice, but circumstances were far from ideal. Fortunately, we had friends and relatives who could help. Chapter 11 contains more details of our wedding. The circumstances of the work I had been doing when I was single did not change much after this great event. I had been working Mother's farm near Silver Creek, Minnesota, since June 1934. Although I had access to the car and bought what I needed from the farm income, I received no wages. Now, the financial arrangements were changed to a 50-50 division of all income and expenses. And I now ate my meals upstairs with my wife instead of with Mother and brothers, John, 15, and Bill, 13.

The arrangements were not the most desirable. We had to share so many things! We had only two rooms we could call our own. If it had not been for the harmonious relationship between Hazel and Mother, there certainly would have been serious friction. But they had a wonderful love and concern for each other. To my knowledge, there was never a cross word spoken in the years we lived in the same house with Mother. In fact, not in the 31 years that Mother lived after our marriage. This is a remarkable and sincere tribute I give to the two people who have meant so much to me in my life.

Fortunately, Hazel and I had gone into marriage knowing that life would not be easy and that lack of money and of many of life's amenities would be our lot for many years. We expected to be happy in spite of that and we worked hard to make it that way.

Hazel and I had not intended to start a family so soon, but we had no regrets when Dr. Bendix told us in 1936 that we could expect a child in September. Hazel had "morning sickness" for months, so she was made distressingly aware of the new life within her.

During the month before the baby was due, I was afflicted

with boils. Shortly before our son Lawrence's arrival, a boil on my arm became infected with a "staph" germ. The doctor told me not to touch Hazel, that the germ I carried was similar to the one that causes childbed fever, which kills so many mothers.

Lawrence was born Sunday, September 13, 1936, about ten o'clock in the evening. He came into the world in the same bedroom in which I had been born 26 years earlier. Dr. Bendix ordered me not even to touch the bed. I was running around with a hot pack on my arm to take out the infection. Antibiotics were not yet available at that time and the doctor didn't take any chances of my infecting Hazel. I was happy that we had been warned of the danger.

Hazel was kept in bed for nine or ten days, which was the custom at that time. Hazel's aunt, Mrs. Ralph Dalman, who was a nurse, was at our home for the first night and day. After that, my mother cared for all the needs of the family as well as the new baby and Hazel.

Lawrence was quite a celebrity upon his arrival. He was not only our first child, but Mother's first grandchild, my Grandfather Mol's first great-grandchild and Hazel's father's first grandchild.

He did not grow well at first and it was soon discovered that he needed more milk than Hazel could supply. When he was given supplemental milk from our cow herd, he soon began to feel better and to increase in weight.

The next years, 1937-39, were years of change in our living arrangements and in our social lives. While brother John was in high school, he went to work for John Schermer, since I did not need both brother Bill and him to help me.

Brother Bill and I were very close during those years as he grew to maturity. In 1938 John graduated from high school and started college in Holland, Michigan. Bill stayed with us until he graduated in 1940, working for other farmers on occasion when I didn't need him.

During this period, Hazel and I made several changes in the house. As Bill and John began leaving home, Mother did not need so much room. Besides, feeding farm help became difficult in our kitchen upstairs. So we divided the large square downstairs living room into a small kitchen, pantry and living room for Mother. That way we could occupy the downstairs kitchen, leaving our room upstairs for a bedroom, as it had been in the first place. There were many other changes, too. A bedroom became a living room, the large storeroom became a bedroom, and so it went, always to accommodate changing situations.

It was during this time that Germany's Hitler was conquering different countries in Europe. Brother Bill teasingly remarked, "Henry is a little like Hitler. Every year he takes another room because he needs 'Lebensraum' [Dutch for "room to live"] as Hitler said he needed for Germany."

In late 1938, when Hazel was again afflicted with morning sickness, we knew that we would be blessed with another child. On June 25, 1939, at one thirty in the morning, our second son, Wayne, arrived. He was ushered in with a lot of heavenly fanfare. Both thunder and lightning announced his arrival. He was born upstairs in the west room which was our bedroom at the time. His face was masked with a grimace as though to say, "I'm not sure I like it here!"

Dr. Bendix and Aunt Marie Dalman officiated at this birth as with the first one. Again, it was around nine days before Hazel was permitted to get out of bed. Wayne was a 10-pound boy at birth, but it took some time before he was able to adjust to this world. His stomach could not tolerate cow's milk very well. Not until the doctor prescribed lactic acid in the milk was he able to digest it properly. We finally bought an icebox and had ice delivered to our door so we could keep the milk cold enough for it to stay sweet. An electric refrigerator was still only a dream for us.

During 1939-51, Mother spent most of her time in Holland, Michigan, where brother John was going to college. She rented a large house and several seminary students boarded at her home. In this manner, she was able to help brother John through college by giving him board and room. She came back here during the summers and sometimes during school vacations. Whenever she was gone from here, we used some of her rooms.

In 1941, my sister Elsie left California, where she had been working, and found work in Holland, Michigan. She also boarded with Mother. Brother John graduated in 1942 and left Holland for Chicago to go to Northwestern Medical School. Mother then moved to a smaller house in Holland and found work in a bakery. She worked there till 1951 when Elsie became too disabled to work. At that time they came back and built in Silver Creek where Elsie died in October 1953. Mother lived there until her death on March 1, 1966.

But to go back a couple of decades or so, as soon as Mother had made her home in Holland, Michigan, Hazel and I were able to occupy the entire house, although we did not make many changes in it until 1946. During the war years, building materials and household goods had been very scarce. Winning the war had demanded all of our country's time, energy and resources.

When Wayne was born, I was 29 years old and still "at risk" for developing ataxia, the heredity disease in our family that causes a degeneration of that part of the brain that controls our coordination. Armed with more information than we'd had in the past, we decided to limit our family until I was 32, past the usual maximum age of onset of that drawn-out fatal disease.

In 1942 we decided to have more children and asked God for a daughter. The onset of morning sickness for Hazel informed us that our wish might come true. At this time we switched to Dr. Raetz from Maple Lake for our medical services. This was not because we were dissatisfied with Dr. Bendix, but it was much more convenient to do so. Our telephone was on that exchange, so we no longer had to pay for a long-distance call. Also, Maple Lake was closer, so we were already using that town as our trading center.

On June 29, 1943, at seven in the morning, our daughter, Marilyn Jean, made her entrance into the world and into our home. My sister Elsie was enthralled. A girl to buy clothes for and to dress up! We were thrilled, too, to have a daughter to grow up with our sons. Marilyn was born in the same room as Wayne had been. I regret that I was not present in the room. Things went more rapidly than we had expected and I was out in the barn milking the cows.

Marilyn was such a lively baby, we did not dare to leave her alone on the table while dressing her. She seemed capable of rolling over on her side almost from birth. I bathed her quite often, as Hazel couldn't be up and my mother was living in Holland, Michigan, at the time.

When Marilyn was about six months old, Hazel was stricken with morning sickness again. She was hemorrhaging and in danger of miscarriage. Dr. Raetz ordered her to stay in bed. We tried to hire a girl to help us but couldn't find one, so I hired Uncle Henry Dalman to do the farm chores while I took care of the family. This was during the winter, so there was no field work to be done.

One morning in March 1944, Hazel woke up and discovered she was hemorrhaging very badly. I quickly found pieces of cloth to soak up the blood, but we realized we had a life-endangering situation on hand. I called Dr. Raetz just as he was leaving his home to go to the hospital in St. Cloud.

He said, "I'll be there as soon as possible. I'll take her to the hospital."

He was there in minutes! I carried Hazel to his car and placed her in the back seat. He jumped into his car and raced off the yard. As they got near Clearwater, Hazel passed out.

Dr. Raetz stopped and gave her a shot of something, then raced on to the hospital, where Hazel was given five pints of blood serum and blood.

Meanwhile, I had to get someone to stay with the children. Uncle Henry could do the chores, but he could not take care of the family. I called Jake Mol and he brought Aunt Ella Mae in a few minutes. I took off for the hospital, not knowing what I would learn. I knew it was serious by the way the doctor had acted. I don't think I ever prayed so earnestly as I did on that trip to St. Cloud.

When I arrived, the doctor told me that the four-month-old fetus had been aborted. All he could say about Hazel was that she was receiving blood and responding well.

That incident should have scared us enough to make us hesitate before considering having more children, but Hazel recovered rapidly and a year later we felt secure in having another. We hoped and prayed that the pregnancy would be normal.

At six o'clock on the morning of January 25, 1946, Hazel started having labor pains. The doctor suggested that Hazel be taken to the hospital. We made some hurried preparations and left for St. Cloud. When we came to railroad tracks in St. Cloud, a long, slow freight train blocked our path. The train backed up, then went forward at a snail's pace.

The labor pains were beginning to come more frequently. I had visions of delivering a baby in a car. After a long 15 minutes, we were able to continue to the hospital. There really had been no reason for concern. Darlene Kay waited until nine thirty that morning to make her appearance. I was not permitted to be present in the delivery room, as I might have been today.

Darlene's digestive system was kind to her and to us. She adjusted to her milk formula quickly. She was a happy baby and grew rapidly. We were a busy family: Lawrence, nine years old; Wayne, six; Marilyn, two, and newborn Darlene.

Hazel sewed many of the clothes and kept the family neat and clean.

In the fall of 1947, Hazel and I knew we were to have another addition to our family. This pregnancy proved a difficult one. Hazel was threatened with miscarriage and was sick quite often. We had many different hired girls come in to help us sometimes for weeks at a time. Hestor, Dorothy, and Thelma Kuiper; Norma and Verna Mae Schermer; Geraline Mol, and Mrs. Dave Bryant were some of them.

Dr. Raetz was again our doctor. In one of his prenatal examinations he said, "I think you may have twins in your womb."

An x-ray revealed he was right. Montgomery Ward's catalogue had a proposition at that time called "twin insurance." If anyone bought a layette from them and there were twins born, they sent the second one free. We couldn't lose, so we sent for the first one.

The babies were due in May 1948, but because of the size and weight, labor pains began the month before. Hazel entered the hospital April 13 and had pain at times, but Linda Lou did not come into our family until two o'clock in the afternoon of April 15. Lois Ann followed in 20 minutes. After the usual nine days, we welcomed home our twins, as we called them for years.

Linda had a special problem. She had to cope with a cleft palate. She could neither nurse nor suck on a bottle. We first tried to feed her milk with a spoon, but discovered that an old nipple with large holes worked the best. The problem that Linda and Lois had with their digestive systems caused us many sleepless hours. Their colic cramps caused them to scream with pain. Many times Hazel and I would each hold one trying to soothe them. They would be about asleep when they would wake up with screams. It took over three months of experimenting with different formulas before they were able to sleep any length of time. These were trying times.

We both had so much work to do and so little rest. It was also very difficult for us to see them suffer so much.

After a few months, Linda was taken to Swedish Hospital for the first of many surgeries to correct her cleft palate. One of the most difficult things for Hazel and me was to leave Linda in that strange hospital with people that neither she nor the rest of us even knew.

After the first few surgeries, she began to realize what was waiting for her and did not want to stay. It seemed to Hazel and me that we could hear her screaming all our way home. It was heartbreaking, but it had to be done. The emotional scars made by all this will, no doubt, remain for the rest of our lives and hers, but it was worth every bit of it. The physical healing that took place after every surgery was just remarkable.

Linda's face and voice became so similar to those of her twin sister, Lois, that only those who really knew them could tell them apart. The love and concern we all had for Linda as she struggled with surgery after surgery made us all very sensitive to the hurts and feelings of others who were handicapped or disabled. Linda's own personality was formed into that of a very sensitive, caring person. The lives of all of our family were made much richer because of the hurts and pains we suffered with her.

In most ways, except for Linda's cleft lip and palate, the two girls seemed identical. It wasn't until the twins were 33 years old that a doctor, while looking into the back of Lois' mouth, mentioned a small slit in her uvula. This might indicate the she has just the start of the same affliction that Linda has, which could confirm that the girls were indeed identical twins.

2

Children's Escapades

As we, Mother and Dad Schut, look back over the years, some memories of our children are good, some not so good. There are no particular reasons why we have remembered certain events better than others. In our busy home with our six children there must have been thousands of incidents worth noting, but we will record only a few samples.

Most boys have a natural curiosity about fire, and Lawrence and Wayne were not exceptions. Despite numerous warnings and threats of punishment if they were ever caught playing with matches, the fascination of flames overrode their fear of reprisal, at least one time for each of them.

One late summer afternoon I caught Lawrence with a handful of matches. He was out behind the henhouse where we used to dump discarded articles. We had dismantled an old car several years before and thrown the gas tank in this area. Imagine my consternation as I saw Lawrence lighting the matches one by one and throwing them into the opening of the gas tank. Fortunately, the gasoline had all evaporated. That scene had every other ingredient of a major tragedy. Besides the obvious danger to him, the tank was leaning up against the wood siding of the building.

A sound spanking and bed without supper was the penalty. After he had cried for quite a time and had made many repentant promises never to do it again, I relented and went to him. I had to let him know I still loved him.

217

As for Wayne, one day he decided to burn up some leaves. That wouldn't have been too serious except for the fact that the leaves were piled up in a basement window well of our house. The blaze grew rapidly and he began to realize the danger. He ran into the house and told Hazel. She promptly extinguished it with a pail of water.

We had difficulty in deciding punishment that time. He had realized and regretted his error and had reported it before any real damage had occurred. We thought he had learned his lesson so let him off with a stern warning.

Climbing is always a handy pastime on a farm. When Lawrence was not more than four years old, we discovered him abut halfway up a ladder that led to the top of our 50-foot windmill. We quietly called to him and told him to climb down slowly and to hold on very tight. In a few minutes the ordeal was over and a couple of grateful parents carried him to the house.

I immediately cut off the rungs of the lower six feet of the ladder. That worked fine at the time, but it didn't prevent the others from trying it in later years. However, the boxes and equipment needed to reach the first rung were usually discovered before the climb up the ladder was in progress.

Marilyn, who was more likely to wander than to climb, gave us many moments of frantic searching. We usually found her after only a short time, but once, when she was around three, she really disappeared! We searched everywhere we could think of. We finally called the neighbors and they helped us look for her, but no Marilyn. After a couple of hours hunting, I noticed the latch on our granary door was unhooked. I gave the various grain bins a quick once over and found her fast asleep in a bin of wheat. What a relief! Of course, she couldn't understand what all the fuss was about.

One story about Darlene that we like to tell and retell happened when the boys were around eight and eleven years old. It was the boys' task to clean the eggs and put them into a

30-dozen case. During the winter, their favorite place to do this was on the floor close to the warm kitchen range. They would place the three-gallon egg pail between them, and the egg case alongside them. A small wet rag was used to clean the eggs.

One evening just before supper, Marilyn, who was about four, was playing and chasing Darlene, who had just learned to walk. They were laughing, giggling and playing near the pail of eggs. As Darlene stepped backwards, she tripped right back into the pail. She landed with her seat in the eggs and her feet and head up in the air. Simultaneous screams and laughter filled the room. It was a hilarious scene, only I didn't see so much fun in it. There were about three or four dozen scrambled eggs lying in the bottom of that pail. Norma Schermer was working for us at the time. She was so overcome with laughter that she could not make supper for quite a while. Hazel had been in another room and came running. What a mess! We lifted the giggling little girl from the pail, raw eggs dripping off her diaper and running down her legs to the floor.

The boys were not shedding any tears either, as their job of washing eggs was suddenly over for the night. There was no way that we could bring about a serious consideration of the value of the many eggs that had become worthless. Looking back over the years, we now consider the memory of the incident priceless.

Linda and Lois came to our home when Lawrence was eleven; Wayne, nine; Marilyn, four, and Darlene only two. Those twins brought us double fun and sometimes double trouble. They were the adventurous type and their main adventure was to get as far above the ground as their little legs and arms could get them. If they could not be found, the best place to look was "up"—up in the trees, up on the top of wagons, up somewhere on the buildings, you name it. They usually ignored the windmill with its cut-off ladder, but as soon as they could pound nails, they nailed boards onto the trunks of trees and then up farther on the limbs. If my tools were missing from the shop, I could usually find them near the place of the twins' latest activity.

An especially pleasant memory comes from a time when I was digging post holes and placing posts in them. Wayne was following me around chatting and asking questions. He was about four years old. As I was on my knees tamping the ground around the post, he came up behind me, put his arms around my neck and sang part of a popular song of the time, "You'll never know, Dear, how much I love you." That is a memory that I shall cherish as long as I live.

When the children were old enough, they brought my lunch to the field in the afternoons. There was always something for them to eat, too, and a sip of Dad's coffee was considered a real treat. When I was picking corn by hand in the fall, they would climb into the wagon near the front where I wouldn't hit them with a corn ear and before long they would be fast asleep. About an hour later, I would have to dig them out from under the ears that had rolled down and nearly covered them. The ride home, sitting beside Dad, made their wait worthwhile.

As the family grew older and the youngsters were in school, the supper table became a time of sharing the events of the day. Mother and I were mostly listeners. Sometimes there was so much laughter that the children just couldn't quit when I wanted to close the meal with reading the Bible or having a prayer. I would try, but a snicker from one would set off a chain reaction of giggles. At times like that, I just decided the Lord knew the circumstances and would understand. Precious memories to cherish!

There were few days without a feud or open battle between one set or another, but the most persistent ones were usually between Wayne and Marilyn. Wayne was the most subtle teaser of the family and Marilyn recognized every movement he made. His every wink or face movement had a meaning (which only Marilyn could interpret) and was cause for a verbal blast or howling complaint.

There wasn't enough room in our home for each child to have a bed, so each one had to share a bed with another. Every bed had an invisible line which was supposed to delineate the boundary between the two occupants. Many battles were fought as one or the other crossed this "no-man's-land." Sometimes it became necessary for a mediator to come from downstairs to settle the dispute.

There usually was a half-hour of pandemonium just before the school bus came in the morning. Four girls and only one bathroom! One morning, one of the girls (which one?) ran out the door with several feet of toilet tissue trailing behind her. Fortunately, one of the others saw it before she got in view of the bus passengers and saved the day.

When the boys were older, milking was a fun time for them and for me. There was constant talking, sharing and laughter. After milking was completed, the boys washed the milkers in the milk house. They often sang and harmonized in many familiar songs. Memories, again, I shall always treasure. My only regret is that the years flew by too rapidly.

When both boys left for college, Marilyn helped me. She carried milk from the cows to the milk tank in the milk house (a task she didn't appreciate very much, I'm sure). But those times were happy in spite of that. I know I did not appreciate the help she gave to me as much as I should have.

Later, the other girls helped only when our hired man, Heinie Thurk, had his time off.

A whole book could be written by their mother about the acts and mistakes of our daughters as she taught them how to cook, sew and keep our home clean. In general, it was Darlene who got involved most with the cooking and baking. The others did more ironing and cleaning.

There were moments of anxiety, too. During the winter of

1947-48, just before the twins were born, all four of the children came down with red measles. We moved beds down to the living room and had them all in one room. Lawrence became quite ill and was taken to St. Cloud Hospital. The others were quite sick, too, but they all recovered without any complications.

In January 1954, Darlene had her appendix removed. That surgery solved several years of urinary infection as the appendix had been attached to the ureter, causing inflammation of the urinary tract.

On August 10-17, 1950, when Lawrence was 14 and Wayne, 11, they each had surgery for hernia. They were in the same hospital room and had very little discomfort, so they used their time to invent ways and means to make the nurses uncomfortable. The whole story of their antics was not revealed to me. I expect it will never be told, at least not entirely truthfully.

It may be of interest to know that Dr. Bendix charged us only $75 each for the surgeries.

Linda was destined to spend many unhappy hours in the hospital. The first surgery on her mouth was done when she was abut three months old. There may have been as many as six or eight operations before she was 15 years old. We regret that we did not record each one as it happened. These surgeries were very expensive, but we received help from the Blue Cross and from the Minnesota State Crippled Children's Fund.

A Dr. Samuel Balkin of the Medical Arts Building in Minneapolis did most of the surgery, at Swedish Hospital. I don't recall ever getting a bill from him. He was a very kind and considerate person, besides being an excellent surgeon.

Lawrence gave us a scare one summer evening in 1950 or 1951. I had asked him to check on the automatic hog waterer we had placed out in a field, and he jumped on the bicycle and started out for it at top speed. It wasn't more than a block away and it should not have taken him more than a minute, but some time went by and he didn't come back. Checking to see why he had been delayed, I found him lying nearly unconscious near the section of new barn that we had built in 1949. As I came near, he sat up and said, "That chicken. That chicken."

The bicycle was lying on its side near Lawrence. As I helped him to his feet, he staggered and rubbed his head and I noticed a large lump on his right temple.

"What happened?" I asked.

"A chicken came running out of that barn door," he said, vaguely pointing to one door of the barn, "and I hit it with the bike. That's all I know."

Going back to where I had found him, I noticed a piece of concrete embedded in the ground, but protruding an inch or more above it. I quickly surmised that Lawrence had been thrown from his bicycle when he hit the chicken, then had hit his head on that piece of concrete.

"Let's get a cold rag on your head," I said.

He didn't seem hurt very badly as we walked to the house. There he lay down on the porch couch where the other children and Hazel also asked him what happened.

Again, all he could say was, "That chicken. That chicken."

We tried to find out more details, but he could not give a clear account of the accident. We let him lie quietly for a short while, checking him often. Before long, he began to repeat things he had just told us. There was no coherent pattern to his conversation.

We became very alarmed and called the doctor. When he came out and examined Lawrence, he could find no serious injury, but said, "He must have suffered a brain concussion. Just keep him quiet and he will be all right."

The next day, Lawrence was all right except for the small wound on his temple and a memory blackout of about an hour after he had hit the concrete. That accident could have been much worse. We wonder at the timing of the chicken's coming out of the door at the exact split second that Lawrence had raced by on his bike. We never asked the chicken how she felt. In fact, we never knew which of our many chickens had made the crossing.

When Linda and Lois were toddlers, they had to spend many hours together in a playpen. They enjoyed each other's company very much and we enjoyed watching them. They never fought with each other until they were 12 years old.

As I may have mentioned before, Wayne began to sing nearly as soon as he began to talk. One Sunday at Sunday School, a visiting missionary asked the youngest class to sing "Jesus Loves Me." There wasn't any response from the class, but four-year-old Wayne agreed to do it alone. He sang the song unaccompanied and in perfect time. The entire Sunday School gave him an ovation.

Marilyn said words at eleven and a half months of age and started arguing before she could even talk clearly. She had banged on the piano since she was four and a half months old. At a year and eight months, we recall, she sat in a bucket of mop water and really soaked herself.

"Official" dating by our daughters was not approved until they were 15 years old. "Unofficial" dating was practiced subtly at an earlier age, I'm sure.

Marilyn's first official date was a memorable one for her, her boy friend and her two brothers. She had long been more than mildly interested in Wayne's best friend, so when his friend showed more than a passing interest in her, she was delighted. The time came when they had a date. They arrived back at our home at a very reasonable hour and parked not far from the house. True to form, Lawrence and Wayne dreamed up a devilish idea. Being good singers and having done a lot of harmonizing, they chose that particular time to do a little practicing on the front porch. The song they chose to sing (about four rods from the parking couple) was an old song popular again at that time. The words were particularly fitting for the occasion—or so they thought. They sang out, "Let me call you sweetheart, I'm in love with you. Let me hear you whisper that you love me, too . . . "

I'm sure Marilyn could have shot them with a clear conscience. Fortunately, the boyfriend later became her husband and the memories have been the occasion for many laughs, but I doubt whether Marilyn has ever entirely forgiven her two brothers for that incident.

Lawrence's dating began in our old 1939 Chev pickup truck. On occasions when he could persuade Dad to trade, he'd have the use of the 1949 Hudson for the evening. At least, he knew that the girls weren't dating him because of his beautiful car.

Wayne had the privilege of having his own car for a time. It was a 1938 Chev coach which had what was called "knee action" on the front axle. This was a good feature until the shock absorbers became worn. Then any bump in the road would cause the front end to bob up and down a dozen or more times. This was particularly noticeable at night because the lights would shoot way up into the air and then plunge down with every bobbing motion. The girls' parents would always know when Wayne brought their daughter home.

3

Footprints into the Future

It was in 1954 that we took our oldest son, Lawrence, to Hope College in Holland, Michigan. That was the opening of a new era in our lives. One by one, each child grew into adulthood and left the home nest to learn to scramble for himself or herself. Only a short time after Lawrence started at Hope College, he added a daughter-in-law to our clan, a precious person named Loretta Klemz.

July 7, 1955, a lovely young lady, Sherry Ann, made us Grandma and Grandpa. Then, on July 14, 1956, a sweet little lady, Maribeth Lou, made us grandparents again.

In 1957, Wayne decided to go to Central College in Pella, Iowa, just to see how he would like it. By Christmas vacation, he had decided to finish out the year and come back and farm with us. However, at the end of the school year he decided to continue college.

In May 1958, Hazel was in the Buffalo hospital. After a few days, Dr. Raetz told us that she had been pregnant and a miscarriage had taken place. Hazel and I had very mixed emotions about the event. We felt our family was large enough, but our children were such a joy to us that we felt sorry that this child would not be a part of our happy family.

In September 1958, it became evident that Wayne was not planning ever to return to the farm. This was where I figure that Wayne's decision perhaps changed the course of our lives

227

as well as his own. I had been operating the farm mostly alone, with Marilyn helping with the milk-ing and by hiring help when it was needed.

Now I began to look for permanent help and was fortunate in being able to hire Henry Thurk before the month was up. He lived in the old house on our east farm, a half mile down the road. He proved to be a very capable person and a great one to work with. Henry Thurk stayed with us until March 1963 when we sold our dairy herd.

In December 1958, the boys came home from college for Christmas. That time was a happy occasion, except for Hazel. She became very depressed and after the holidays, on January 5, 1959, she was taken to Glenwood Hills Hospital where she was partly under my brother John's care and was treated by Dr. Garvey.

Hazel remained there until January 30, when she returned home. However, she did not improve very much and returned to the hospital on February 11. She received six electric shock treatments before returning home again on February 18. She was quite confused for a few weeks, but she slowly improved to her normal self. Her memories of some events were erased by those treatments, but most of them returned over the passing years.

On December 9, 1959, Ronald Lee arrived into the home of Lawrence and Loretta. We were grandparents for the third time!

Ever since I was forced to quit college in 1934, I had dreamed of completing my college career. The urge became stronger as I saw our children graduate from high school and go on to college, until in January 1960 I entered St. Cloud College. At first I helped on the farm while Henry Thurk did most of the farm work. But in March 1962 I finally felt that it was possible for me to receive a degree in teaching, so that's when we sold our dairy herd. Henry Thurk left to work at William Mol's garage.

I operated the farm during the summer and raised some hogs and young cattle.

In June 1962, Lawrence graduated from medical school.

In December 1963, I received my degree. I started teaching in the public school at Kimball, a town about 20 miles west of Maple Lake. That was in January 1964. In September of that year, I started teaching in Upsala, Minnesota, driving to St. Cloud where another teacher, Mrs. Pat Ditlenson, and I took turns driving the remaining 35 miles to Upsala.

A year later, in September 1965, I began teaching in Maple Lake Public School, where I taught until my retirement in June 1975.

This change in my occupation had a very great effect on our daily schedule. Instead of the milking and other farm-life time schedules, we had to adjust to the school schedules. The only regret I have about making this change is that I wish I had done it earlier in my life.

Leaving a profitable farm operation for an uncertain future in teaching may have seemed stupid to many people. At times it did to me. But the support and encouragement I received from Hazel and our children were very helpful in keeping me motivated in times of doubt and disappointment.

In September 1961, Marilyn entered St. Cloud State College where she completed one year. On December 29, 1961, she added a son-in-law, John N. Lee, to our growing clan. I could write pages on the blessings and pleasure that he brought to our family, but those close to us who will read this will know what I mean.

In June 1961, Wayne graduated from Central College and decided to continue his education at New Brunswick Seminary in New Jersey. The following year he married his college sweetheart, Joyce Van Roekel. After two years, he was convinced that God was not calling him to be a pastor, but rather to help the physically and emotionally handicapped.

On June 5, 1963, Wayne and Joyce presented me with a

unique birthday present—a granddaughter named Lynn Renee.

At the end of that year, on December 17, 1963, Steven John Lee arrived at John's and Marilyn's home. Grandpa and Grandma again!

September 1964, Darlene left the home nest to attend Central College in Pella, Iowa.

May 13, 1965, a young man named Michael Wayne arrived at the home of Wayne and Joyce.

On December 3, 1966, I was hospitalized in the Buffalo hospital until December 12, 1966. This was the first of a series of blood circulation problems which have put me in the hospital many times. I'm not sure, but I think Dr. Raetz was my doctor.

In 1966, Darlene told us there was a young man from New Jersey who wanted to become a member of our family and that she and Edward Scott wanted to make it official and permanent on August 19, 1967. We were happy to accept one of the best of the East into our family clan.

On March 1, 1966, Grandma (Jennie Schut) was called home to be with the Lord.

In September 1966, Lois entered Augsburg College in Minneapolis, and Linda, the Swedish Hospital nursing school, also in Minneapolis. That left Hazel and me with a very empty house, but a family that had grown in number to 19.

On December 24, 1967, a young lady was born in Bethany Home in Michigan. She was chosen to make her home with Marilyn and John who adopted her and named her Lori Ann.

On January 16 through 19, and again on January 22 through 24, 1968, Hazel was in St. Barnabus. She had a complete examination: EKG, complete x-ray, brain scan and other tests. This was the result of a cancerous growth on the outside of her skull. The tests were done to make certain there were no other growths in her body. All tests were negative.

In June 1968, Darlene graduated from college and moved

with her husband to Monroe, Iowa, where Ed was teaching.

The 1960s had certainly been years of change for our family. While the children were busy getting an education, Hazel had been dreaming about a new house. Her dream came true July 4, 1968, when we moved into our new home, a 14-year-old house that we had movers bring from Minneapolis to our east farm, just a quarter mile east of my birthplace.

In the years 1964 to 1968 we had raised some steers on the crop-share money that we received from renting our land to Myron Johnson. We rented the west farm home to different renters, but the land was rented by Myron Johnson until 1975.

We continued to raise some steers at the new homestead while I was teaching in Maple Lake.

On January 12, 1969, a blond little "Dutch" girl named Katrina Elizabeth arrived in Wayne's and Joyce's home in Cuttingsville, Vermont.

From January 22 to 26, Hazel was in St. Cloud Hospital with bowel problems which recurred again April 7 through 11, 1969, when she was again hospitalized and treated with various drugs until it was cured.

On April 30, 1969, a dark-haired young lady was born, also in Bethany Home in Grand Rapids, Michigan, and on July 29, 1969, John and Marilyn adopted her, the first brunette to enter our family clan. They named her Jodi Kay.

In the summer of 1961 Linda completed her Registered Nurse's degree.

The 1970s started rather calmly, but on May 11, 1970, (Lawrence) James Jr. created a splash when he came into the home of Lawrence and Loretta. Soon after, Lois received her teaching degree from Augsburg College.

The calm was broken many times in this decade when a number of illnesses struck both Hazel and me.

The years had been kind to us in so many ways. I had been spared the disease ataxia, and Hazel had recovered from two serious miscarriages and a depression. All of our children except Lois had had surgery and recovered. But the years were taking their toll. On November 28, 1971, I suffered a heart attack and spent 11 days in the hospital. Later examinations revealed two arteries in the heart to be restricted.

In the summer of 1972 we went to Holland.

In the fall of 1972, Hazel had a series of depression episodes which finally hospitalized her in St. Cloud Hospital.

On December 3, 1973, I had heart surgery and had two by-passes put in the arteries of my heart. Just a few weeks following this surgery, Lois brought another teacher into the family when she married Chuck Bakker. With him we welcomed two step-grandchildren, Derek, born in 1968, and Kyle, born in 1970.

The 1970s were marked with my hospitalizations and Hazel's several more depression periods, which did not require hospitalization. These periods came in four-to-six-month cycles, alternating between her feeling very well and then quite depressed.

In 1975, as I have said, I retired from teaching and began substituting in the area schools. That same year Darlene's and Ed's first child arrived on July 10. Almost one year later to the day Charles Henry (Charlie) was born to Chuck and Lois.

On May 30, 1978, Hazel was suddenly released from the depression she had been in since January of that year. She has remained emotionally stable since then.

On September 4, 1978, Aaron, a brother to Amy Scott, was born. Charlie Bakker was also joined by sister Keri on Valentine's Day, 1979.

I had successful prostate surgery in June 1979.

Hazel had a hysterectomy in February 1980.

On January 20, 1980, our daughter Linda was united in marriage to Doug Foster, another fine young man to add to our family.

I had glaucoma surgery on my left eye in March of that same year.

There have been many events, too numerous to mention, but the pleasant ones I have included will give some idea why I have always considered ours to be a happy family. Those that were not so pleasant could, I suppose, give any reader a "pain in the neck."

We have now reached 1981 with many parts of our bodies repaired, some replaced, some missing and many not working properly, but we are thankful to God for sustaining us through these 45 years of our marital pilgrimage.

On May 6, 1981, our dearly beloved father, Henry, was taken home to the Lord, following complications from a triple by-pass. The memories of our father are very dear and will always be treasured. After his death our family has continued to grow.

Doug and Linda's first child, Jason, was born on July 7, 1982, the last of the grandchildren.

The death of Steven, Marilyn and John's only son, in 1986, at the age of 22, was a great loss to us all.

Now the older grandchildren are marrying and adding great-grandchildren to the family. They will carry on the great heritage passed down to us by our ancestors.